THE COLUMBIA

SUSTAINING A MODERN RESOURCE

THE COLUMBIA

SUSTAINING A MODERN RESOURCE

TEXT AND PHOTOGRAPHS BY TIM PALMER

A JON BECKMANN BOOK

Published by
The Mountaineers
1001 SW Klickitat Way, Suite 201
Seattle, WA 98134

10 9 8 7
5 4 3 2 1

Published simultaneously in Great Britain by
Cordee, 3a DeMontfort Street, Leicester,
England, LE1 7HD

Manufactured in Hong Kong by Bookbuilders, Ldt.

Copyedited by Deborah Kaufmann
Illustrations and maps by Jim Hays
Photo on page 47 by Glenn Oakley. All others by
the author.
Cover design by Watson Graphics
Book design by Alice C. Merrill

Cover: *Columbia River Gorge and Crown Point,
Oregon.* Photo by Dennis Frates
Half title: *The Columbia Gorge*
Title page: *Winter in the Gros Ventre Range*
Frontispiece: *A remote section of the upper Kootenay
River in the Canadian Rockies.*

Library of Congress Cataloging-in-Publication Data
Palmer, Tim
      The Columbia River : sustaining a modern
resource / Tim Palmer
      "A Jon Beckmann book."
          p.   cm.
      Includes biblipgraphical references and
          index.
      ISBN 0-89886-474-7
      1. Stream ecology—Columbia River
Watershed. 2. Pacific salmon fisheries—
Columbia River Watershed. 3. Forests and
forestry—Columbia River Watershed. 4. Land
use—Columbia River Watershed. 5. Nature,
Effect of human beings on—Columbia River
Watershed. 6. Columbia River Watershed.
I. Title.
QH104.5.C64P35   1997
333.91'62'09797—dc21   97-12007
                                                            CIP

Contents

Storm clouds gather over the Sawtooth Mountains. Here at Redfish Lake, the headwaters of the Salmon River collect and then flow across Idaho to become one of the Columbia's important tributaries, vital to salmon and steelhead.

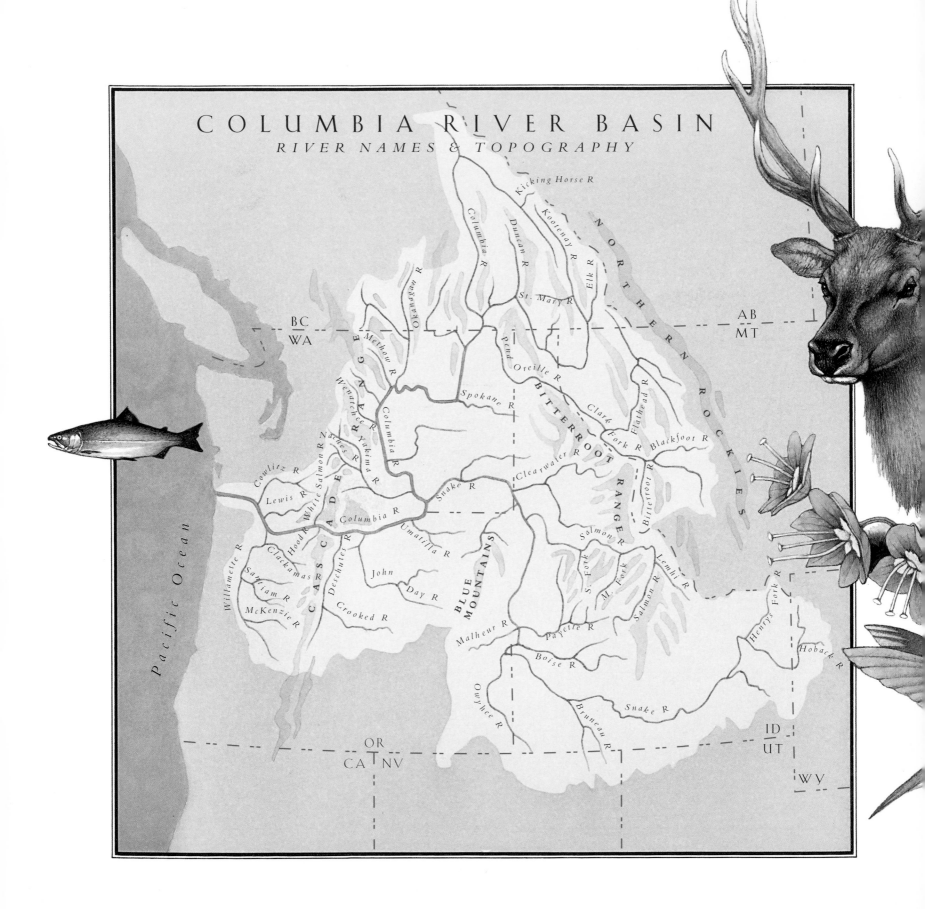

COLUMBIA RIVER BASIN
RIVER NAMES & TOPOGRAPHY

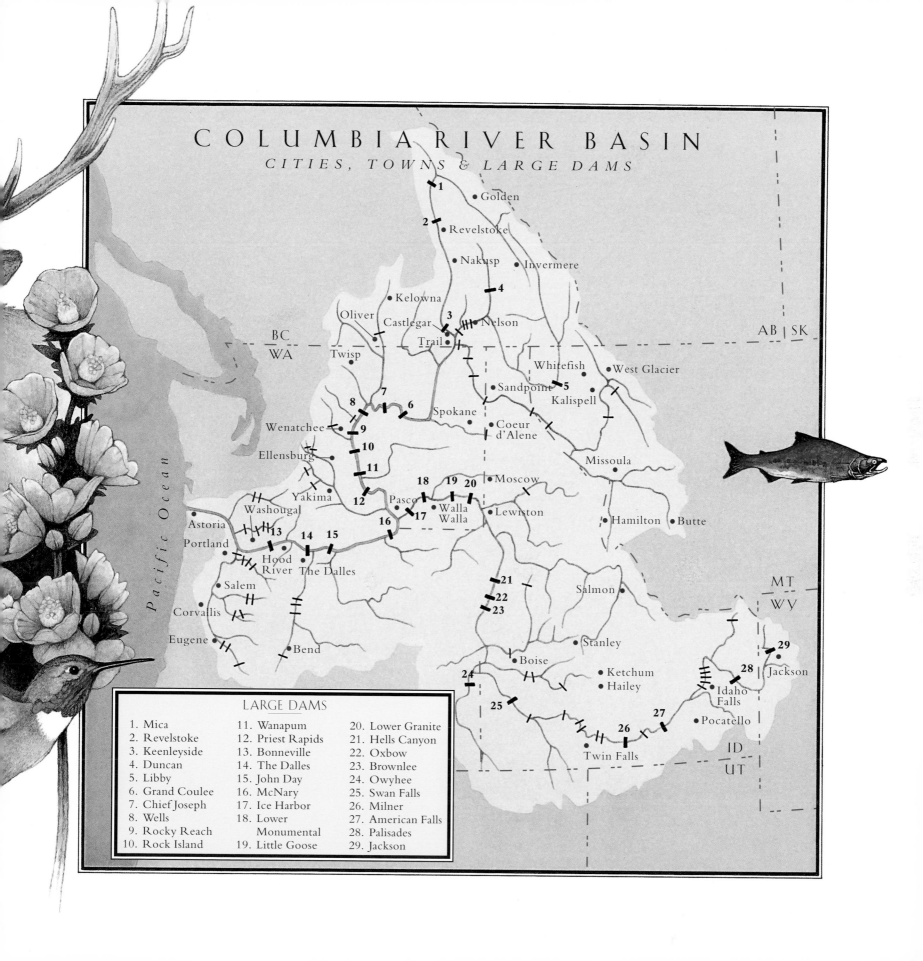

COLUMBIA RIVER BASIN
CITIES, TOWNS & LARGE DAMS

BC
WA

AB | SK

MT
WY

ID
UT

Pacific Ocean

Golden
Revelstoke
Nakusp
Invermere
Kelowna
Oliver
Castlegar
Nelson
Trail
Whitefish
West Glacier
Twisp
Sandpoint
Kalispell
Wenatchee
Spokane
Coeur d'Alene
Ellensburg
Missoula
Moscow
Yakima
Pasco
Walla Walla
Lewiston
Washougal
Hamilton
Butte
Astoria
Portland
Hood River
The Dalles
Salem
Salmon
Corvallis
Stanley
Eugene
Bend
Boise
Ketchum
Hailey
Jackson
Idaho Falls
Pocatello
Twin Falls

LARGE DAMS

1. Mica	11. Wanapum	20. Lower Granite
2. Revelstoke	12. Priest Rapids	21. Hells Canyon
3. Keenleyside	13. Bonneville	22. Oxbow
4. Duncan	14. The Dalles	23. Brownlee
5. Libby	15. John Day	24. Owyhee
6. Grand Coulee	16. McNary	25. Swan Falls
7. Chief Joseph	17. Ice Harbor	26. Milner
8. Wells	18. Lower	27. American Falls
9. Rocky Reach	Monumental	28. Palisades
10. Rock Island	19. Little Goose	29. Jackson

A PLACE OF GREAT CONSEQUENCE

—⟨∞⟩—

Ancestors of today's Indians knew it well: Nch'i-Wána, the Great River. *Columbia* was simply part of the name given to Bostonian Robert Grey's ship, which he sailed into the mouth of the river in 1792. The name was derived from that of another explorer who had journeyed from Spain to the Caribbean exactly three hundred years earlier. But the word now rings with its own sound, bigger than life. *Columbia*. It resonates with majesty and mystery. It alludes to an overflow of natural wealth in the Pacific Northwest, and certainly to power—river power and the derivative hydroelectric power. After seven generations of white settlement, the name Columbia still excites people from coast to coast with near-mythic visions of hearty salmon, ancient forests, and mist-shrouded mountains. Such is the past. But what is really there, today?

Flowing from seven states and one Canadian province, drawing on a hundred mountain ranges and a thousand tributaries, the Columbia River's watershed reveals not only the wealth of two nations but also unconscionable losses in the wake of a civilization that takes with little restraint from everything it touches.

This book, *The Columbia*, focuses on the modern river we have inherited from those who by money, might, and popular appeal dominated the decisions affecting all residents, all creatures, all waters, and even the atmosphere we breathe. Many dramas are now being acted out in the grand epic of this place, and so *The Columbia* considers not only the main-stem channel of the river—principally a chain of dammed-up reservoirs—but the whole fabric of the watershed.

My own involvement dates to 1967 when I hitchhiked to a summer job with the National Park Service. Every weekend, I traveled and saw as much of the land as I could, sometimes not returning until the workday began on Monday morning. Like many people, I was attracted and fascinated by what I found. Like many, I wanted

LEFT: *Wapta Falls on the Kicking Horse River thunders like Niagara in the heart of the Canadian Rockies.*

RIGHT: *At the Yakima River headwaters, the east side of the Cascade Mountains drains into the Columbia, whose sprawling basin covers parts of seven states and one Canadian province.*

FAR RIGHT ABOVE: *A Yoho River tributary races with glacial runoff, which later feeds the young Columbia in Canada.*

FAR RIGHT BELOW: *Rafting, canoeing, and kayaking are ways to see and explore remote reaches of the Columbia's tributaries. This rapid lies in the Middle Fork Boise River.*

to come back or stay. Two years later I worked as a seasonal landscape architect for the Forest Service at the headwaters of the Salmon River, a place that went straight to my heart. Over the years I returned as if drawn like a spawning salmon to that and other magnetic sites in the Columbia Basin. British Columbia became my favorite vacation destination. In 1988, when I began writing a book about the Snake River, I journeyed to the upper reaches of that largest tributary, where I have spent winters ever since.

Many of us have an attachment to a place we call home, or we've adopted a plot of earth that draws us back again and again. For me, the entire Columbia watershed is a place I have yearned to know well. It is a region of great consequence to all its residents and one of symbolic and real importance to many Canadians and Americans.

This river and its land are strikingly different from the rest of the United States and Canada. Dams block the Columbia more than any other large waterway on the continent; even the back-to-back dammed Ohio has headwaters with substantial free-flowing length. In contrast to other landmark rivers of the West, large portions of the Columbia Basin receive heavy snowfall and rain. Thus, while the Colorado, Rio Grande, Arkansas, and Platte Rivers are diverted and depleted of their flows, the Columbia funnels water by the billions of gallons to the sea. Along with the Columbia, only the Klamath River of Oregon and California cuts through both the Cascades and Coast Range of the Northwest, though the Klamath is small by comparison. To the Columbia's north, the Fraser

River of British Columbia is a virtual twin, but through the diligence of Canadian conservationists, has escaped the barrage of dams.

Underscoring the river's importance, the Columbia ranks as the fifth largest river on the continent, fourth largest in the United States, and largest draining into the Pacific from the western hemisphere. Running with an average of 265,000 cubic feet of water per second (cfs) at its mouth, it is exceeded only by the Mississippi with 593,000 cfs, the Saint Lawrence with 348,000 cfs (a river that is also shared with Canada), the Ohio with 281,000 cfs flowing into the Mississippi, and northwestern Canada's Mackenzie with 280,000 cfs. The north-south dimension of the land drained by the Columbia equals the distance from Chicago to the Gulf of Mexico; east to west, the Basin would extend from New York City to Chicago.

The weighty volume of the Columbia translates into importance of many kinds. The river system, including thousands of streams and creeks, is of legendary biological abundance, supplying water for six million people who live in the Basin and generating power in America's largest hydro-electric system, which produces an average of 18, 500 megawatts in both countries—enough to serve 70 percent of the greater Northwest. The complex of dams, reservoirs, penstocks, turbines, and wires results in the lowest electric rates in America. Because the power is cheap, the use of electricity in the Northwest is the least efficient in the nation. A lot of energy is wasted.

The Columbia Basin means water and power, life and money, but even more fundamental to the national psyche, the lyrical sweep of land here inspires people to plan big and live hopefully, as it has since the explorations of Lewis and Clark.

Their party of twenty-five men and one essential Indian woman entered the watershed over Idaho's Lemhi Pass. Pressing northward in this last quadrant of the United States to be explored, the group traversed the Bitterroot Valley, then turned west and crossed Lolo Pass near today's Missoula. Compelled to eat horses, the explorers might otherwise have perished in early winter snowstorms. Descending to the Clearwater River, they entered a valley of welcoming warmth and friendly Indians who gave them food, guided them, and even retrieved a runaway canoe from a rapid. Lewis and Clark proceeded by dugout down the Snake River to the Columbia and out to the ocean beyond today's town of Astoria. They called the nation's attention to a magnificent abundance of salmon, a humbling overstory of trees so immense as to be scarcely imaginable, and a landscape as varied as that of a whole continent, from blistering desert to mildewing woods where in wintertime rain drenched the earth for weeks.

Within forty years, "Oregon Fever" had gripped the adventurous and malcontent in Eastern and Midwestern states, and farmers were cramming all they could into wagons bound for the Willamette Valley of Oregon. In this first mass migration to the West, settlers scrambled against all odds to reach the Pacific side of the Cascades, where a new life awaited—or so they thought. Oregon was the chimera of a better existence, and in that sense the eclectic migration once pulled by oxen, horses, and mules was not so different from what continues today in Fords, Toyotas, and U-Hauls. Weary urbanites seek new breath in the flowered city of Portland or the many attractive towns from Walla Walla to Whitefish, Sandpoint to Bend.

The promise of a good life with home, health, and natural heritage explains much of the change occurring in the Columbia watershed today and marks this region as a heartland of hope. But no less important, the lands drained by the Columbia include features found elsewhere. The craggy peaks of the Bitterroots, the desert of the Owyhee, the ponderosa pine of the Flathead and western red cedar of the McKenzie, the orchards of the Okanagan and dairies of the Willamette, the urban hum of Portland and roadside sprawl of Spokane—this catalog of landscapes could well describe a whole continent in scaled-down size.

Think about what might have happened here if America had been settled from west to east rather than east to west. Portland might be more of a New York or Philadelphia, and the Columbia might be more of an Ohio River lined from culm bank to slag pile with industries. Settlement of the West Coast had a one-hundred-year delay that might be considered a late start down the road of

industrialization or a century-long reprieve, depending on your point of view.

Today's watershed paradoxically contains the wonderful and the awful. Here lie some of America's cleanest streams, but also the vilest toxic waste dump at radioactive Hanford. Some of the largest old-growth forests can be found on Cascade slopes, but muddy clear-cuts also checker the mountains like the grid of cornfields in Iowa. Development in booming times seems to press as hard on the Basin as the weight of water against Bonneville Dam. Everything people can do to the land is done in this formerly paradisiac region of the West. But compared to other places similarly rich in water, soil, and living space—California and Florida, for example—the Columbia remains a stronghold of open space. With a land ethic in mind, the possibility of doing better is real. There is still time. We don't have to make all the errors we've made elsewhere, blunders that today send refugees fleeing to the Northwest in hope of escape but, unfortunately, without enough determination to avoid creating the same problems they flee.

In keeping with its role as a heartland of hope and a destination for people seeking a better life, the Columbia watershed ranks high with an inventory of intrinsic qualities valued by people. Salmon, a traditional source of food, pulse up and down the rivers like the beat of the region's heart. Here were once the most numerous runs of salmon in the world. On tributaries to the Columbia, young salmon still drift down and out to sea where they spend several years growing into lustrous, muscled adults up to four feet long. After foraging as far as the Gulf of Alaska, they return to the mouth of the Columbia, evade the commer-

Streams of the Columbia Basin have supported a vital commercial and sport-fishing industry but are threatened by habitat destruction. This brown trout is being released in Silver Creek, Idaho.

cial fishermen and predators at sea, slip past Indian fishermen in the rivers, climb up fish ladders in an effort to circumvent eight major dams on the Columbia-Snake route, swim through hundreds of miles of flat reservoirs where water temperatures peak at threatening limits, and then press onward to spawn in the same swatch of gravel in the same small stream where they were born. Because of dams, habitat loss, and the unintended but insidious effects of artificial hatcheries, many runs of wild salmon are already extinct and the remaining populations imperiled. Restoring some of the natural assets of the Columbia is a prerequisite to the survival of the salmon.

Of comparable importance, the woodlands on the Pacific side of the Columbia Basin are emblematic of ancient forests in America. The spotted owl, marbled murrelet, and other endangered species depend on old-growth stands of two- to eight-hundred-year-old timber for their existence. While the loss of these creatures may be significant, the vital message of this strife-torn chapter in environmental history is not that owls will die out but that we've changed the face of the earth so much that whole groups of creatures can no longer exist. The difficulties faced by the owl indicate that an entire ecosystem has been ravaged. Is this our idea of multiple use, sustainable use, or wise use? To many people, the ancient forests are what makes the Columbia Basin and Northwest so special. Only here can we protect a final remnant of the growth that once existed across much of the continent.

Even with the losses, the Columbia remains a place of hope for Americans and Canadians, for newcomers and natives. Though information is

important, knowledge alone will not save what is worth saving. The necessary ingredient is that of living here with the excitement that comes from seeing a wild fish and with the joy of walking through an ancient forest. The essential bond is the one that people make with the land when they stop to listen and care.

The Saint Joe River watershed once contained some of the finest old-growth forests remaining in the Rocky Mountains, but timber companies are cutting them at a rapid rate.

CHAPTER ONE

ONE WATERSHED

FROM THE ROCKIES TO THE PACIFIC

While dozens of tributaries remain wild enough for wolverines, the Columbia's source suffers a different fate. In southeastern British Columbia, the river begins in a wetland, fenced in as a pasture for cows. A highway skirts one side and a puffing, clanking, hardworking sawmill lies just out of sight. In its first mile, with peaks of the limestone-rooted Canadian Rockies soaring skyward to the east and the granitic Purcell Mountains immediately west, the river telegraphs a message about its persistent character: a wonderland of nature feeds a river that is processed and rebuilt from end to end.

One end, at the Continental Divide in the Rockies, and the other, surfside at the Pacific, are connected by this river in a landscape of superlatives. So sensational, diverse, and far-flung is this Basin across 259,000 square miles that to each familiar place-name a person might respond, "That, *too?*" What Yellowstone National Park and

LEFT: *The Little North Santiam River near Opal Creek survives as a natural refuge and a reminder of the wildness and crystal clear water that only 150 years ago were found in much of the Columbia Basin.*

Portland, Oregon have in common is that they are both drained by the Columbia. Likewise Missoula and Eugene, the North Cascades of Washington and the Jarbidge Mountains of Nevada. The sand that sticks to your feet at the Clatsop Spit on the Oregon Coast could be from Mount Sir Donald in British Columbia or the South Sister in Oregon. The river is the common denominator, the ultimate sink, the central engine room of economy, and the shared heart-line of biology.

Canada's Selkirk Mountains and central Oregon's Cascades are each a part of the water-shed just as veins, arteries, and the heart are all parts of the same body. And at the Columbia, nature's circulatory system of water nourishes every form of life. Being there day-to-day, we see only fragments of this geographic organism. This chapter aims to examine and seek the importance of each place and the connections that stitch together these neighborhoods of mountain, forest, and desert into one watershed with a future common to everyone.

Looking at the entire landmass drained by the Columbia, I see that in the most simplified sense, the Basin is shaped like an upside-down Africa, and can be viewed as seven pieces that fit together as if part of a jigsaw puzzle made for a child.

As the first piece, the Rocky Mountains form the headwaters in a land of forest and rock, from the icefields at the border of Jasper National Park to the Wyoming Range near the Utah state line. With wildflower high country at its crests, this eight-hundred-mile-long, north-south backbone of the continent bulges westward across central Idaho and, in Canada, the Selkirk and other

mountain ranges join the Rockies in a continuous rugged mass.

The second piece, as extensive as the first, is the Columbia Plateau of dry and sometimes desert land that occupies the interior and south-ern Basin, including the Palouse Hills of northeast Washington, the Channeled Scablands of east-ern Washington, the Yakima Valley of central Washington, the Snake River Plain of southern Idaho, and isolated ranges such as the Blue and Owyhee Mountains of eastern Oregon, which rise like islands above a dryland sea.

The other five pieces of the puzzle are smaller, their combined acreage totaling about 30 percent of the Basin. The third piece interlocks with the desert region at the northwestern margin of the Basin, where the glacially bulldozed North Cascades send their runoff to the middle Columbia. The fourth contains the giant volcanic peaks of southern Washington's Cascades, which descend from snowy heights to shady forests and feed the Yakima River and Columbia Gorge. The Oregon Cascades, the fifth piece, lie in an elegant chain to the south. The sixth, paralleling the Cascades, is the pastoral Willamette Valley and its guardian hills, which form the watershed's south-western border. The final piece of the puzzle is the low breach in the Coast Range where the Columbia, with runoff from the whole Basin, drifts out to sea.

Draining these contrasting landforms, the Columbia and its feeder streams pass through them all, from timberline to valley floor. The river and its tributaries connect the Basin together in a web of flowing water, the central organizing principle for understanding the Basin. To better experience the entire Columbia, I started my travels at the source of the river and followed its path downstream from the Rockies to the Pacific, noting where each major tributary joined and exploring many of those side streams as I went.

The Upper River

To begin at the beginning, in Canada, I drove to the Columbia's languid headwaters at Canal Flats, a marshy lowland where the river starts its wrap-around course to the sea.

Dramatically sited, the upper Columbia lies within the Rocky Mountain Trench, a continuous lowland formed by faults that runs one thousand miles along the base of the Rockies from the Liard River in northern British Columbia to the Mission Valley in Montana. Deep in the moutains, this place once formed the Pacific seashore; the Columbia River didn't even exist. According to plate tectonics theory, 175 million years ago the westward drifting North America collided with a separate, floating portion of the earth's crust that geologists call the Intermontane Terrane, which buckled up to form the Columbia Ranges. With the creation of these and other westward mountains, including the volcanic Cascades and seismic Coast Range, the runoff of the Rockies was forced into a tortuous route to sea, and a drop of water at the source of the Columbia now has 1,248 miles to go before joining the Pacific.

Here at the upper reaches of the river, the most grandiose of all water projects was proposed, in the 1960s, to capitalize on the geology of the Rocky Mountain Trench. The boosters of unlimited development in southern California who called themselves the North American Water and Power Alliance saw the possibility of diverting

rivers from British Columbia and even Yukon Territory southward through a dammed-up Trench, and then dispersing their liquid gold to half the United States for irrigation and city water supplies. With opposition from Canadians and American conservationists, the plan was exposed as, literally, an engineer's pipe dream; it became obvious that economically feasible water sources were more easily available through efficiency improvements, the retirement of unproductive irrigated land, and the development of closer sources. A more feasible scheme to divert the nearby Kootenay River into the Columbia was also defeated by a Canadian citizenry informed about the biological and hydrological consequences of drying up one great river and perpetually flooding another to produce hydropower unneeded in Canada.

The unexpected route of the Great River—north, then south, briefly east, at last decisively west—surprises people today no less than it did in 1811 when David Thompson, a Canadian explorer, first charted the Columbia's length, but only after years of humbling trial and error. He had to launch several expeditions, giving up when he should have kept going and starting again in his effort to follow a river course that detours around entire mountain ranges and slices straight through others like some cartographer's practical joke.

At 2,650 feet above sea level, the river's source at Canal Flats soon empties into Columbia Lake, a windswept oval of whitecaps fifteen miles long and a mile wide. It aims northward beneath shadowy mountain peaks. Below the lake's outlet, where the current whisks water away, the stream does not enter the wilds of B.C. as might be expected here, sandwiched between two of the great mountain ranges of the West, but flows through a golf course. You can smack a ball across the river at several different holes. Fairmont Hot Springs, fully developed, attracts world travelers just up the hill. At the bridge, in stark contrast, stroll elderly people in tourist clothing while log trucks hurricane by at fifty miles per hour snorting fumes and spitting bits of bark. WATERFRONT HOMESITES are advertised on big signs, and swank vacation retreats fit for the California coast border the greens. Fairways line the riverbanks, and a riprap of rock, dumped on shore by the developer, bosses the diminutive channel, already a servant of commerce.

But not for long. Leaving golf carts behind, the Columbia enters its second natural lake, Windemere. At its northwestern end, the flowery town of Invermere invites the visitor to lounge on the shore or sail beneath airy peaks. Lazy and lakeside, it's difficult to think of beach life on Windemere as the Columbia, but it is. Ospreys, nesting in town neighborhoods, make a living by fishing in the river.

At the lower end of Invermere, I set my canoe into the water, packed it full of gear at the head of the river's longest remaining free-flowing reach, and kicked off from shore. For the next 108 miles, from Windemere's outlet to the town of Donald, which consists of a large sawmill, one of the finer river and wetland complexes on the continent shimmers across the valley floor. This liquid land glistens in a kaleidoscope of braided river channels, backwater sloughs, ponds, lakes, cattail marshes, and natural levees of silt, all whining with billions and billions of mosquitoes—a bug mass so thick it deters all but the hardiest birdwatchers.

Confined to the Trench, the Columbia here jogs left and right but lacks the broad, sweeping meanders typical of low-gradient streams. From my open vantage point in the middle of the Rocky Mountain Trench, peaks of the Canadian Rockies' Main Range escarpment receded one behind another, upstream and downstream; dozens of summits were visible all the time in a mountain mass that eventually receded beyond the curvature of the earth. I spotted five black bears in one day, all drawn to the river's edge to forage on red osier dogwood berries that had just fleshed out. Bald eagles roosted singly, in pairs, and in screeching threesomes so plentiful I quit counting on day two. The upper Columbia remains a wetland paradise, much as the great rivers of the Midwest existed before drainage, channelization, and damming. The province owns much of this waterfowl haven while other tracts are held by rural residents and ranchers, some of whom have mowed down the floodplain's richness for pasture and a few of whom would like to mow more. Taking part in a provincial land planning effort, a local group called the East Kootenay Environmental Society strives to protect nature's 64,000-acre sponge as the great wetland it is.

Scores of mountain streams tumble into the river, reminding me about what is going to happen: the little Columbia is going to grow and grow, until no one will ever believe it was once little. With each tributary, the river's flow builds, from mountain stream to full-bodied river to continental giant. I regarded the mouth of each tributary as the portal to another room, to another watershed. Each was fascinating in its space and contents, in its offer of refuge and prospect, in its enticement to enter and explore a new enclave of

the Columbia Basin. At each tributary I wondered, *What will I find?*

None is more enticing than the healthily flowing, 1,448-cfs Kicking Horse. At Golden it joins the Columbia, now a hundred yards across and 5,500 cfs on average. Golden is known as the third most timber-dependent community in the timber-dependent province of British Columbia, but a fundamental fact of life has changed. The old-growth timber is nearly all cut. The town thrives anyway, having avoided the gutted-out, saloon-lined main streets of has-been logging towns elsewhere in the West. With style and grace, people here seem to be making the transition to a recreation-based economy. It helps that Yoho National Park lies at Golden's doorstep, and that the provincial government in the 1990s supported local communities in becoming attractive places to live.

The Kicking Horse riffles through the center

The uppermost reach of the Columbia is the longest of only three main-stem sections that remain undammed.

of Golden. Fascinated by its milky flow and wondering where it came from, I left the Columbia for a while and drove toward the tributary's headwaters with my wife, Ann, who had shuttled our van down from Invermere, camping on her own for three days. Now speeding along with both tourist and transcontinental truck traffic, we rolled up through canyons and forests to the high country.

While the canine-toothed Tetons, stormy-souled Selkirks, and snow-cone heights of the Cascades all rise as breathtaking crowns of the Columbia watershed, no other mountains possess the massive and utterly perfect grandeur of the Canadian Rockies. Their forested lowlands of blackened green, layer cakes of sedimentary rock, and saddles and side slopes of blue glacial ice set them apart. The eons have compressed marine-deposited sediments into long, narrow bands of rock, sharply folded and faulted. Thousands of years of glacial activity produced broad, U-shaped valleys of textbook cause and effect clarity; unlike the V-shaped cross section of canyons eroded by water, the solid but slowly creeping mass of ice scoured wider trenches with broad floors and curved sides. The western slope of the Continental Divide—where the Kicking Horse and Columbia flow—is markedly warmer and wetter with dripping Pacific air masses compared to the eastern slope, which faces the frigid interior of the continent where nothing but a stunted boreal forest stands in the way of winds from the North Pole.

Originating at the heart of the Canadian Rockies, only one ridge away from the postcard-familiar Banff and Lake Louise, the upper Kicking Horse River is bolstered by flows of the zesty Yoho, which means, loosely translated from the Kootenay language, "Wow!" Streaked with current, the milky

Yoho is full of swift-water bubbles and the rock-flour of glaciers that grind down the earth and excrete a pulverized dust that, combined with sunlight, dazzles the eyes in brilliance. The river is white! The Yoho churns down into gorges so steep and narrow you can't see into them. After joining the Kicking Horse, the water braids across ice-carved, gravel-filled valleys flat and wide. Tucked into the mountain slopes, the town of Field served as a historic railroad siding where engineers coupled extra engines onto their trains chugging up the Rockies. The settlement is now headquarters of Yoho National Park, formed in 1886—one of the world's first national parks, established only fourteen years after Yellowstone. The Kicking Horse rages over Wapta Falls, eighty-nine feet high but Niagara-like in dramatic stature, reached only by trail. The river finally speeds through thrilling and sometimes impassable canyons to its Columbia confluence in Golden.

Downstream from town, where I again set off in my canoe, the Columbia Valley undergoes its first great botanical change. The grassy woods of ponderosa pine and Douglas-fir deepen into a moist forest of red cedar and hemlock, which continues to Castlegar, forty miles north of the international boundary.

Still a youthful river, with only 11 percent of its mileage behind it, the natural Columbia prematurely ends twenty-three miles below Golden where the terminal free flow curves decisively west and the current spins into flat-water eddies of the uppermost of fourteen reservoirs. Kinbasket Lake sprawls behind the 650-foot Mica Dam, capable of containing 20 million acre-feet of water. America's tallest dam, by comparison, is Oroville, on the Feather River in California, an

Brilliant waters of the Yoho River rush down through a national park—one of the protected gems of the Canadian Rockies.

earth-filled, 770-foot-high structure, but it impounds only 3.6 million acre-feet of water. Mica flooded an eighty-nine-mile-long empire of prime forest in 1973. Enough lumber for 100,000 homes was salvaged from the reservoir area but at least an equal amount of forest remains in a watery tomb. The flooded forest might still be logged, not by scuba-equipped lumberjacks but with remote control saws and tree grippers run from a boat.

The dam is a two-and-a-half-hour drive from the nearest town via Highway 23, which bridges dozens of tributaries in which waterfalls on the right side of the road rush to their demise in the reservoir on the left. The wild streams come from a summit-cresting wilderness that fingers down to the Columbia River Valley—once the central artery of all life but now the biologically dead bottom of the ecosystem where the reservoir's shoreline fluctuates through 180 vertical feet of muck and rotting stumps. Swaths of clear-cut forest extend for miles along the shores and expose whole naked mountainsides.

About this scene, realtor Julia Cundliffe in Golden reflected, "We were promised so much with the dams. Thirty years ago people didn't think about conservation or the river. We didn't know that the 'recreational lake' would be fluctuating in its level, its shoreline covered by mud and dead trees. And there seemed to be no choice; this is what the government was going to do. No one realized that land in this part of the country would be so valuable today." Taking a province-wide perspective on what Cundliffe described, Mark Angelo of the Outdoor Recreation Council of British Columbia said, "The Columbia dams stand as a testament to the damage we can wreak

on a river if it is viewed primarily for hydroelectric value."

A few downriver towns now enjoy flood control, and B.C. Hydro (the provincial utility) generates 1,736 megawatts of electricity on its best days at Mica. But the real business of all the flooding by

Mica Dam is the first of fourteen impoundments on the main stem of the Columbia. The spillway here drops 650 feet to the river valley below.

the Canadian dams has been to provide a steady flow of water for power generation at United States hydroelectric plants. The Columbia River Treaty of 1964 required that three dams be built in B.C. for water storage, making possible added generation at downstream dams in the U.S. Half of the total stored water on the main stem of the Columbia lies in B.C., and 3,000 of the river basin's 18,500 average megawatts are produced there. In exchange for its land, rivers, wildlife, fisheries, farms, and homes, the province was paid $64 million by the United States. By treaty, half of the power from the additional generation in the U.S. belongs to B.C. The province sold this "Canadian entitlement" to the Bonneville Power Administration (BPA) and southwestern utilities for a one-time fee of $254 million, good for thirty years because the power was not needed in Canada. The combined payments covered most of B.C. Hydro's costs of building the dams.

In a mania of nature-conquering in mid-twentieth century, both countries wanted the Columbia River to be dammed at any cost, but now the politics get interesting. The initial agreement will expire in 1998. Renegotiation has been a contentious process, with BPA in 1995 backing out of a nearly done deal that provided for American use of 500 megawatts for a one-time cash payment of $180 million to British Columbia. The amount of power to be returned to Canada would be permanently reduced from 1,450 to 950 megawatts. The BPA, a part of the U.S. Department of Energy, believed it had to cancel that agreement when a glut of electricity appeared on the Pacific Coast in the mid-1990s. If no other agreement is made, BPA by treaty must send the full entitlement back to Canada. The treaty, however, requires that the power be returned to a remote site called Oliver, selected in 1964 not because of anyone's desire to have electricity delivered there but simply out of desperation to finalize the treaty quickly. Rather than have BPA build new powerlines through easily damaged terrain and further add to a surplus of electricity in B. C., the province wants to receive all of its entitlement at a site in Oregon near John Day Dam, with the freedom to sell it to American customers. If this plan fails, and the power is returned to Canada, the province wants it to go via existing wires to the Vancouver area—a cheaper and less damaging solution for everybody. BPA, fearing competition for its own customers, resists both Canadian proposals and threatens to build the high-voltage line to Oliver. This ploy may simply be a straw man to enhance BPA's bargaining power over issues of megawatts and money. The outcome of these sticky international negotiations is unknown at the time of this writing.

After thirty years of resentment from the people of the upper Columbia Basin, the British Columbia government has established a Columbia Basin Trust, governed by people of the headwaters region, to invest funds received from power sales. These will be spent on social, environmental, and economic development projects with the intent of reimbursing local people for some losses incurred because of the upper Columbia River dams.

Immediately below the base of Mica Dam, flat water of the second reservoir backs up the Columbia without so much as one intervening riffle. Completed in 1984, Revelstoke is one of few large dams that was constructed after the dam-building era of 1930–1980 had ended. Ninety-three impounded miles of the southbound river reach to the mountain-ringed town of Revelstoke. There the splashing Illecillewaet River joins the Columbia after foaming down from the Selkirk Mountains, cloaked with 412 glaciers in one of the more extreme jumbles of rock and ice in North America. In the high country, thirty-two feet of snow and a lot of rain fall during 213 days of precipitation a year. The crowning peaks are in Canada's Glacier National Park (which is completely separate from Glacier National Park in Montana).

Trails here switchback up wooded slopes to alpine meadows and then to the scraped rock of newly glaciated ground, a raw-boned island of topography, all of it surrounded by the Columbia and its tributaries. Hiking here, alone in the cool days of September, my nerves buzzed with the anticipation of encountering grizzly bears feeding on the rich mix of berries, roots, and grubs.

Near the mouth of the Illecillewaet, Arrow Lakes Reservoir backs up nearly to the foot of Revelstoke Dam and extends through 144 miles of forests and clear-cuts southward to Keenleyside Dam. This third and final blockage on the main stem in Canada required the relocation of 2,000 people before it was completed in 1968, flooding the beautiful Upper and Lower Arrow Lakes.

Through its westward and then southward course in British Columbia, the river lies impounded for a total of 326 miles of flat water, which makes less evident the contribution of hundreds of tributaries that drain numerous glaciers and pour like huge open faucets into all sides of the three big reservoirs. Accumulated water blasts from the gates at Keenleyside Dam—70,000 cfs here exceeds by far the volume upriver at Mica. When I stood on top of the dam, it felt as if a continuous earthquake was underway.

Immediately below Keenleyside, the monolithic Celgar Pulp Company lines the right bank with several running miles of sky-probing smokestacks, an obstacle course of railroad tracks, chips and sawdust in piles resembling sifted flour, conveyer belts toting burly logs as if they were sticks, and tree-lifting thongs that could pluck a bus from the highway. Dioxin discharges that contaminated fish for nearly two hundred miles have reportedly been eliminated in recent years. Below the mill, the hearty Columbia of deep, swirling green brushes past the town of Castlegar and receives its first megatributary.

An extraordinary water course in its own right, the 480-mile Kootenay begins in the glaciated Canadian Rockies of Kootenay National Park and flows through stellar canyons and braided channels in high mountain valleys. Below Canal Flats, its whitish blue glacial waters brush within two miles of the source of the Columbia, and then ease southward. Below the confluence with the Saint Mary River, the Kootenay matures in biological health, otters, eagles, osprey, and waterfowl are common, but then pools into the reservoir of its first dam. Called Koocanusa—a concatenation made up by boosters combining the words Kootenay, Canada, and USA—the American dam backs up water for ninety forested miles through Montana and British Columbia.

Spelled Kootenai in the U.S., the river drops over the screaming cataract of Kootenai Falls, the only waterfall remaining undammed or undiverted on the exceptionally large rivers of the American Rockies (other high-volume waterfalls once existed on the Missouri, Pend Oreille, Snake, and Columbia). Below the sawmill town of Troy,

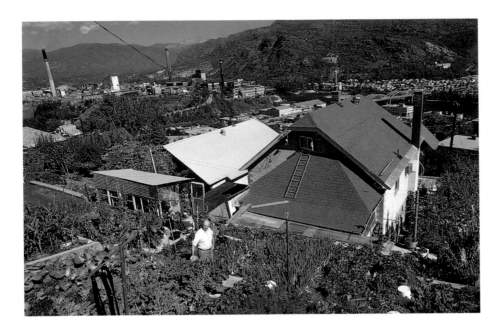

In Trail, British Columbia, the maturing Columbia flows past the behemoth Cominco smelter, far below the backyard garden of Angelo DeGrandis.

From Keenleyside Dam to the backwaters of Grand Coulee Dam in Washington, the current runs fifty-five speeding miles. A deep, spacious, forceful flow, the river of lucid green rips past rocky shoals that in some places congest one side of the river or the other but never form really fearsome rapids. Here is British Columbia's finest rainbow trout fishery and best habitat for white sturgeon. But the proposed Murphy Creek Dam, above the town of Trail, would put a quick stop to fishing by flooding the trout spawning beds with flat water. Another B.C. Hydro dam near the U.S. border would add to the losses, but both are on hold owing to excess power, opposition from anglers, and recent B.C. policies emphasizing energy efficiency. Proposed hydroelectric generation upriver at Keenleyside Dam also threatens to alter flows and deplete the trout and sturgeon populations, but B.C. fishing groups are fighting to control the damage.

broad riffles where I've run carefree canoe trips lead to the loggers' town of Bonner's Ferry, Idaho. Once-great populations of white sturgeon—the largest freshwater fish in North America—are now on the road to local extinction owing to Koocanusa with its flooding and manipulation of downstream flow.

The Kootenai drifts northward and back into B.C. to face five dams, one right after the other through low, wooded mountains. It receives the heady flow of the Duncan River, which draws on Selkirk glacial wilds before being impounded by yet another dam built under the U.S.-Canadian Columbia River Treaty. The Slocan River also runs to the lower Kootenay after leaving its striking, undammed, headwaters lake and flowing through rapids and pools in a temperate valley of log cabins and vegetable gardens where just the sight of the place made me want to live there.

Returning to the Columbia right above the Kootenay confluence, I launched my canoe in the second free-flowing reach of the Great River.

Halfway through the free-flowing section, the burg of Trail rises on adjacent hillsides crisscrossed by narrow streets. With tin roofs for snow protection in winter, pedestrian stairways zigzag up tough grades. Ann and I climbed to the top and gazed out over hundreds of colored rooftops to the valley, the river, and unavoidably the smelter. This small town is dwarfed by the largest zinc and lead plant in North America. The industry came here because of cheap hydropower; it uses enough electricity to fuel a city of 250,000. Slag banks veer up at their angle of repose from the swift water's edge, up to smokestacks that pump eye-stinging clouds into the sky and to behemoth buildings that rattle and shake as trainloads of ore are dumped, fired, and processed into metal for American and Canadian car bodies and plumbing fixtures.

Noxious smoke at Trail was so bad that Americans, twenty and more miles away, brought the case to the International Joint Commission in 1927, predating most air pollution concerns. Sulfuric acid was reduced by converting the waste to fertilizer, but ammonia, mercury, cadmium, arsenic, zinc, and other hazardous wastes remained problems. Toxins once dumped wholesale into the river still contaminate fish behind Grand Coulee Dam, 170 miles downstream. Advisories were issued against eating more than eight ounces of the delectable walleye per week. The Cominco Company's daily disposal of 400,000 pounds of black and contaminated slag continued until 1995 and still coats beaches with coal-like granular waste from here to Grand Coulee's backwater, where it smothers bottom life on the bed of the reservoir. In the 1970s Cominco faced the decision to move or remodel. The company decided to stay, and spent $1 billion replacing an old zinc smelter with a new, cleaner one. Smoke still curls out of the stacks, but workers are building a lead smelter that will eliminate more of the contamination. Proud of their identity, the high school hockey team here calls itself the Smoke Eaters, and its insignia proclaims the belching stacks.

Unlike grimy mill towns of the American East that have a similar profile of age, steep hillsides, and European ethnic diversity, Trail is a bright and alive hub of 12,000 people. Steady income from the smelter keeps the economy moving, and the air emissions cleanup has no doubt improved the health and appearance of the town. The main streets hop with business, and the homes, anchored into hillsides, are painted and tidy. Lead contaminates the soil to the degree that children should not play in their native dirt, but people still grow

gardens of vegetables and flowers that color the town. Longtime resident Angelo DeGrandis, who cheerfully greeted us as we strolled past his home, showed us his basketball-sized cabbages, squashes that would take a week to eat, and tomatoes as big as grapefruits, all of them fattened on fertilizer he imports to his hillside garden.

Below Trail, turbulent water boils with short rapids welling up in frightening force, driven by a pushy flow with sucking undertows. The forested countryside dries out; ponderosa pine and juniper indicate that I am easing toward the desert of Washington's Columbia Plateau. Then, only seventy-five yards before the international border, the Pend Oreille River enters the Columbia.

As the second big-volume tributary, twenty-eight miles below the mouth of the Kootenay, the Pend Oreille is called the Clark Fork in its upper reaches in Montana. The Clark Fork/Pend Oreille is the longest river lying within the Rocky Mountain region of the United States. The 580-mile system exceeds the main-stem Columbia above the confluence, but in volume, the Columbia is several times larger; it rains and snows far more to the north. The Clark Fork (not to be confused with the Clark's Fork of the Yellowstone, which lies east of the Continental Divide) begins far to the southeast near Butte, Montana, and for 120 of its headwater miles sadly constitutes America's longest Superfund toxic waste site. Heavy metals from a century of copper mining and smelting lace the riverbed and floodplains in northwestern Montana. The effect is one of putting the Trail smelter along a stream you could skip a stone across, rather than along the diluting flush of the brawny Columbia. The Montana smelter was closed in 1980. The related copper mine, which was devouring the town of Butte in big bites of open pit that literally step off into a yawning hole from the central business district, was closed in 1983, leaving no jobs and a legacy of waste for today's Montanans.

The best features of the Clark Fork are its tributaries. It picks up the scenic waters of the Blackfoot—the setting for Norman Maclean's novel, *A River Runs Through It*. In Missoula it also meets the cottonwood corridor of the Bitterroot with its Huck Finn getaway of islands. Then the Clark Fork passes through rapids and dams on its way to the Flathead River.

The Flathead's exquisite North Fork of blue-green water and riverbed of red, white, black, gray, and blue stones scribes the boundary of Glacier National Park. One of the classic parks in America, this mountain landscape is a southern extension of the Canadian Rockies and maintains all their character of grand views, dizzying drops, and glaciated plateaus roamed by grizzly bears, white-bearded mountain goats, and bighorn sheep. To the south, the Middle Fork of the Flathead flows from even wilder country in the Bob Marshall Wilderness complex of 2.5 million protected and unprotected acres. Likewise, the South Fork comes from wilderness before encountering Hungry Horse Dam. The Flathead basin illustrates some of the best of nature in the Columbia Basin.

Swollen with the volume of the Flathead, and now in drier country of ponderosa pine and tawny bunchgrasses that are unfortunately invaded by the exotic knapweed, the Clark Fork flows into Idaho and bellies out into Pend Oreille Lake. Though forty miles long and bolstered by a dam, the lake is only a token of its ice age size. A sea of glacial meltwater called Lake Missoula lay here as recently as 18,000 years ago and stretched from Sandpoint, Idaho, southward to Hamilton, Montana—two hundred miles. With all northern outlets blocked by ice, the lake filled until it ruptured its natural dam and spilled repeatedly in one-thousand-foot-deep floodwaters of unimaginable fury across eastern Washington. Dry Falls at Grand Coulee was the world's largest waterfall, two times as high and five times as wide as Niagara with forty times the volume. Today's Pend Oreille Lake empties into the back-to-back dammed Pend Oreille River. Once a rapid-filled, high-volume artery through uninterrupted ancient forests, the Pend Oreille is now harnessed in hydropower dams to its mouth, where one lonely, remaining rapid jets into the Columbia.

Back on the big river below the Pend Oreille confluence, the Columbia exits Canada, a country where 40 percent of the river's length drains 15 percent of the total watershed and contributes 38 percent of the Basin's water. In volume, the Columbia as it leaves Canada ranks second only to the Fraser among the rivers of British Columbia. Less than halfway to the ocean, the Columbia's average volume of 101,300 cfs here makes it the fifth largest river in the United States; it already exceeds all but the Mississippi, St. Lawrence, Ohio, and Yukon.

THE MIDDLE RIVER

As it enters Washington State, the Columbia eases past the onetime smelter town of Northport and through a final small gorge into Lake Roosevelt, the reservoir that lies behind the monumental Grand Coulee Dam. Molded in art deco slabs of

Grand Coulee Dam generates enormous amounts of hydroelectricity but floods 137 miles of river valley and blocks salmon from 1,000 miles of spawning habitat that once reached to the headwaters of the Great River.

concrete by engineers during the Depression, and completed in 1941 as one of the first great megaprojects in water development, this Bureau of Reclamation plug in the Columbia backed up the water for 137 miles and consumed more concrete than any other structure on earth (other dams and reservoirs, however, are larger). Diversions irrigate 500,000 acres of the Columbia Plateau desert, and the dam can generate 3,492 megawatts of electricity—the equivalent of three nuclear plants. Without seriously considering fish passage facilities, the Bureau of Reclamation eliminated 1,000 miles of salmon habitat by building the dam. One-hundred-pound chinook called June hogs once swam to the river's Canadian headwaters but, without fish ladders, all anadromous, or sea-running, species were stopped.

Surrounding the reservoir, northeastern Washington is mostly dry, rolling country with scattered forests and plains. The Columbia's principal tributary here is the Spokane River. As its source, the Saint Joe River riffles from the splendid forests of northern Idaho, a totally green landscape of corrugated mountains. The famously clean water of this gravel-bottomed lifeline is now suffering from a rapacious era of timbering; in the mid-1990s, when I last camped in the valley, log trucks rumbled down the remote highway at a rate of three per minute.

The Saint Joe eddies into the southern side of Coeur d'Alene Lake while the Coeur d'Alene River fans into the eastern end. This small stream meanders through expansive floodplain wetlands near its mouth but is laced with lead, cadmium,

Rolling hills of the Palouse country in eastern Washington and northwestern Idaho are fertile but easily eroded when the plowed soil is washed by rains.

and zinc from past and current silver mining that has excavated huge chunks out of the pine-clad mountains. While businessmen in the fine resort town of Coeur d'Alene downplay the problem at the festive urban lakefront, local Indian tribes are trying to get money for reclamation and to require mining companies to fix the damage. In 1996 the U.S. Department of Justice brought a pollution case against eight mining companies.

When the rivers flow out of Coeur d'Alene Lake's dammed outlet, they are renamed the Spokane, which riffles through progressively drier country to sprawling Spokane, an urban area of nearly 400,000, the second largest city in the Columbia Basin. In the center of town the river crashes over a basalt waterfall, is dried up at a hydroelectric diversion, and then resupplied in rapids before a long reach of lower river where reservoirs back up against each other down to the Columbia.

Here in eastern Washington, lava oozed across the region many times about 13 million years ago, each layer up to seventy-five feet thick. Then, about 18,000 years ago, the release of glacial Lake Missoula caused the Bretz Floods, which attacked this starkly bizarre landscape, stripped the topsoil, and scoured canyon-depth trenches to create the Channeled Scablands. Floodwaters created necklaces of lakes and wetlands, including the choice waterfowl habitat at Turnbull National Wildlife Refuge south of Spokane, which appears incongruously amidst the eastern Washington drylands. Lying outside the route of the Bretz Floods, many other square miles of eastern Washington roll in a nearly sensuous softness under deep, fertile, wind-blown soil called loess, which originated as silt deposits left over from the glaciers, as floodplain

silt that had dried out along glacial rivers, and as volcanic ash. Cultivation easily erodes these rich soils; for every bushel of harvested wheat in the Palouse region, 1,400 pounds of topsoil wash or blow away.

Sometimes on the surface and sometimes underlying the loess, the basalt crust of plateaus and buttes stretches southward through Washington, western and southern Idaho, and central and eastern Oregon except for the granitic tips of a few mountain ranges such as the Blue and Wallowa, which peaked above the apocalyptic flood of encroaching lava. Like claws of a giant paw scratching this landscape of volcanism, the Columbia and its tributaries have scraped dozens of canyons into the basalt bedrock.

Entering the other side of the mid-Columbia, to the west, the Okanogan River flows quietly in a fruit tree valley through northern Washington and southern British Columbia, where the river is spelled Okanagan. Because of intensive agriculture and development pressures, coupled with a temperate climate where north meets south and wet meets dry, the Okanagan watershed is a hotspot for British Columbia's endangered species. Biologists struggle for ways to protect shrinking habitat in one of the most sought after regions of Canada for retirement living—a sunny retreat for refugees from the rain of the Vancouver area.

To the south, in Washington, the Methow River plunges off the North Cascades, a range housing North Cascades National Park and most of Washington's one thousand glaciers, which comprise 95 percent of the total in the U.S. outside Alaska. The North Cascades' extreme relief and glacial activity left hanging valleys of sweeping grandeur, as well as cirques, arêtes, and U-shaped trenches that could almost be Switzerland but fortunately lack the ubiquitous Alp railroads and cable cars. Ambitions to really see the mountains here can be thwarted for days and weeks by gloomy, gray weather and cold, biting rain. But the climate creates a high country of incredible green, amazing to see if you are lucky enough to be there when the clouds part and the fog lifts.

Southward, Lake Chelan lies as a fifty-five-mile-long flooded trench penetrating deep into mountain goat terrain with the Stehekin River as its source in a green and white geography of trees, waterfalls, and snow, a river so cold that the quickest dip makes your scalp ache. Farther south, the picturesque Wenatchee River courses down from the mountains with crushing flows in Tumwater Canyon. To the delight of tourists, the old logging town of Leavenworth deliberately rebirthed itself as a Bavarian mountain village, offering all the travelers' amenities of restaurants, hotels, and shops. One of the significant wilderness regions of the nation, this corner of Washington retains two roadless areas of over a million acres each, interrupted by only one highway between the Canadian border and Stevens Pass, west of Wenatchee—a mountain-crested distance of 115 miles as the crow flies. Lower reaches of these North Cascades tributaries along with the mid-Columbia and Yakima Valleys form the heart of Washington's balmy orchard country, which leads the nation in apple production and also grows peaches, plums, cherries, and pears.

The middle Columbia of central Washington is blocked by seven dams below Grand Coulee. Chief Joseph, Wells, and Rocky Reach Dams are followed by Rock Island—the oldest main stem

Columbia River dam—built in 1932 by the Puget Sound Power and Light Company. Wanapum and Priest Rapids are the final dams in this cluster.

Out of six hundred Columbia River miles above tidal zones in the United States, nearly all are dammed into flat water. Lacking both a current and a sequence of pools and riffles, and without a riparian corridor of cottonwoods and wetlands along its banks—and with a total makeover of its biology from prolific river life to sparse reservoir life—the Columbia is not a river anymore. A profile of the river is now a stair step of bloated impoundments where for hundreds of miles the monotony of currentless water is broken only by another dam with its humming power plant and buzzing wires leading off to Seattle, Los Angeles, and Albuquerque. Where Indians once spearfished for salmon at the base of thundering drops called Death Rapids, Priest Rapids, Kettle Falls, Celilo Falls, The Dalles, and the Cascades, reservoir water now englooms the riverbed to

The Hanford reach of the Columbia is the only free-flowing section of the river remaining in the United States and is vital to the survival of salmon.

dark and spooky depths. Lewis and Clark wrote of places below the mouth of the Snake River, where salmon swam thick and whole colonies of otters thrived. The river remained wild until 1932, but instead of a river, we now have an average firm power supply of 14,670 megawatts—roughly what New York City consumes. The river has been replaced, and with it has gone much of its chain of life. Above tidal zones, in the United States only one piece of the flowing Columbia remains.

Below Priest Rapids Dam lies the final of the Columbia's three real river sections—a fifty-two-mile, free-flowing reach crossing the desert to Richland. But for thirty-five miles through the Hanford Nuclear Reservation, the Department of Energy posts both sides of the river against entry. One of the most sinister of all American landscapes, Hanford housed the development of atomic weapons and plutonium production in a science fiction architecture of cube and dome structures attended by machine-gun-armed guards and linked by rail, power, and water lines from the Columbia.

Waste from these facilities has been carelessly stored and dumped into so many ditches that nobody remembers where they all are. Radioactive strontium-90 has leaked into the river at nine hundred times the standard for drinking water, 120 square miles of aquifer have been polluted, and hundreds of accidents have occurred. The Department of Energy called Hanford "the single largest environmental and health risk in the nation." Projected government cleanup costs run from $50 billion to $1 trillion, and the work will take thirty years or more. Even if that happens, most people recognize that the desert here will

never be fully reclaimed. From 1988 to 1996, $8 billion were spent on cleanup with almost nothing to show but studies and more estimates. Plutonium production was stopped at Hanford in the late 1980s, but the legacy of our forty-year experience with nuclear weapons is an intractable and costly problem that could plague future generations for 200,000 years—you might say forever.

In the fall of 1995, the Department of Energy reported that one principal contractor, Westinghouse Hanford Company, had charged taxpayers for emergency drills that never were held, spent money on unnecessary repairs, and otherwise performed in ways that, according to the Department, were "less than satisfactory." While reducing the budget on cleanup, congressional conferees even in this post–Cold War era approved $2 billion—an increase of $250 million—for other nuclear weapon development programs serving a vast private industry of nuclear contractors. Another $20 million a year for Hanford's public relations escaped the budget ax.

The waste from Hanford hasn't seeped into the river alone; it has blown across towns and farms as well. After World War II, people living downwind from Hanford were exposed to 5,500 curies of radiation—ten times more than what some people living near the Chernobyl disaster of 1986 were exposed to. One-fourth of the people living near Hanford's worst area during the exposure have died of cancer since the 1960s. Apparently unfazed by the downside of nuclear weapons, the Richland high school athletic teams call themselves the Bombers, their proud logo being a mushroom cloud like the one over Hiroshima that killed 64,000 civilians—more than all American deaths in the entire Vietnam War.

The bomb means big business in the nearby Tri-Cities, where the economy and radioactive waste are rationalized in the name of national security. Doing anything they can to keep the pipeline of federal dollars flowing, local government officials in Benton County sought an injunction against the Department of Energy from shutting down operations such as the $100 million per year Fast Flux Test Facility, which had no use, current or projected.

Radioactive problems at the Idaho National Engineering Laboratory in the desert of the upper Snake River in Idaho are less severe than at Hanford but also of great concern. This sister facility in nuclear weapons production has leaked radioactive isotopes in large doses into the groundwater, which inexorably heads for the river. Governor Phil Batt in 1996 opened the doors to eastern Idaho as the nation's waste colony for some of the most troublesome and toxic substances known. In contrast to both Washington and Idaho, the Oregon legislature and governor passed a law banning the storage of nuclear waste anywhere in the state.

Ironically, the 560-square-mile Hanford reservation has remained virtually undisturbed except for the nuclear facilities and dumps, which occupy only 5 percent of the arid land. Being off-limits to everybody, the rest of the site holds some of the least disturbed sagebrush-steppe landscape remaining in the West: a broad prairie of bunchgrass, sage, and rare desert plants on rolling hills cut by springtime drainages, all of it a home to coyotes, deer, and screeching red-tailed hawks. With Hanford's nuclear responsibilities being phased down, local counties want the land deeded to them so they can sell it for more irrigated farming. But the Yakama

Indian Tribe wants part of the land to be returned to their reservation, and much of the acreage is ideally suited for wildlife refuges.

Even more ironic, the Hanford reach is the one remaining spawning area for salmon in the entire main stem of the Columbia. The river's gravel beds constitute some of the most critical habitat of the entire watershed. Seen from a canoe floating through that quiet desert with white bluffs to the east and gravel bars in the shallows, the Columbia still feels powerful, primal, and alive.

A reservoir, of course, was proposed here. Boosters for Ben Franklin Dam can still be found, but their case for spending hundreds of millions of taxpayer dollars to serve a few minor shippers of surplus grain in the town of Wenatchee has lost favor, and the project will likely not be built. The Army Corps of Engineers' alternative was to dredge the river for a shipping route and thereby kill off the salmon by channelizing their habitat rather than damming it. Meanwhile, the Department of the Interior has found the reach eligible for National Wild and Scenic Rivers designation, which would ban the dam and the channelization for good. With antigovernment rhetoric, local interests have stalled the proposal, though it poses no threat to private property.

At the bottom end of the Hanford reach, the Yakima River joins the Columbia. Bringing a whole different set of assets and problems to the Basin by linking Cascade splendor, irrigated farmland, and the bleached-bone desert of central Washington, the Yakima runs for two hundred miles. Headwaters of the Cle Elum sing through a mountain valley scented by fir. The Yakima's upper farming valley, called Kittitas, houses the college

by twenty-three dams, including one in Grand Teton National Park, three in the upper half of Hells Canyon, and four in the lower river. This artery drains western Wyoming, far eastern Oregon, southwestern Washington, and a sliver of Utah and Nevada, but most of the watershed lies in Idaho.

The undammed sections of the Snake flow as remarkable reaches, including wild mileage in Yellowstone National Park and the classic of river and mountain scenery at Grand Teton National Park. Below Jackson, Wyoming, Alpine Canyon is one of the three most-paddled gems of white water in the West with 162,000 floaters in 1995. Downstream, in the parched desert of the middle Snake, Shoshone Falls is higher than Niagara, but irrigation diversions reduce the deafening cataract to a pathetic, algae-scum trickle through much of the year. At Milner Dam, three river-sized canals shunt the water away to irrigate the Snake River Plain in a grid of crop-filled fields for eighty miles across southern Idaho. Farming is a way of life here, but erosion from agriculture has cut the productivity of the fertile Snake River Plain by 25 percent, according to Department of Agriculture studies. Greater care of irrigation systems and runoff is recommended. Farm towns such as bustling Twin Falls and quiet Hagerman grow with an influx of people drawn to the hot and sunny climate and to small-town life along the river and at the rim of its canyons.

town of Ellensburg—an American dream of small-town life. The Naches River pours in just above the growing city of Yakima, headquarters of Washington's most productive farm region, extending almost to the mouth of the river near Richland, Kennewick, and Pasco. There, from the opposite shore, the Snake River also merges into the Columbia.

THE SNAKE RIVER

The Snake packs more than its share of remarkable geography into 1,059 river miles—126 miles longer than the Columbia above the confluence but carrying only 30 percent of the flow after the two join. Still, this largest Columbia tributary delivers 56,900 cfs and ranks as the twelfth largest river in America. It begins in Yellowstone National Park, but half of the Snake's mileage is impounded

The Snake recovers from the irrigation diversions only when Thousand Springs pours a river's worth of accumulated water from fractured basalt walls that are dotted with hundreds if not literally a thousand springs. Below there, on golden desert cliffs, the Snake River Birds of Prey National

Conservation Area houses the greatest concentration of nesting raptors on the continent. Farther downstream, beyond the farmed valleys and a hundred-mile-long complex of Idaho Power Company dams at the Oregon border, Hells Canyon ranks as the second deepest canyon in America, exceeded only by the Kings of the southern Sierra.

Tributaries to the Snake describe a who's-who of wild and valuable rivers in America and drain dozens of mountain ranges in the northern Rockies and Columbia Plateau. From the west side of the Tetons, anglers regard the Henrys Fork as America's premier dry-fly river. The Wood River riffles past Sun Valley. Below there, water that is not diverted for hayfields disappears underground to reemerge as the spring-fed Malad River, which joins the Snake in southern Idaho. The Bruneau saws into a phenomenally narrow, vertical-walled canyon of hard basalt in southwestern Idaho, and farther west, the Owyhee carves a similar path through the rugged desert of Idaho and Oregon. These canyons lie as yawning gulfs etched into the basalt plateau, and those who are not shocked are at least surprised when they step up to an unexpected canyon rim on a plain otherwise as unbroken as Kansas.

The Malheur River flows from the snow-corniced height of Steens Mountain in Oregon and the waterfowl magnet of Malheur National Wildlife Refuge, then drains a watershed over-grazed by cows. Heavily diverted, its remains finally trickle into the Snake. The Boise and Payette Rivers in central Idaho begin as glimmering streams of the Rockies with high-country views and cottonwood-willow corridors, then graduate to rapid-studded reaches before flatten-

ing out in drylands and joining the Snake. The beautiful Imnaha of white water, grassland savanna, and evergreen forests drains the isolated block of the Wallowa Mountains in northeastern Oregon—a miniature Rockies of granite peaks and snowfields surrounded by dry country.

Greatest of all Snake River tributaries and a highlight to the entire Columbia Basin, the Salmon River is America's longest nearly un-dammed river outside Alaska that also flows without major diversions (a weir, amounting to a small dam, blocks the headwaters' reach at a federal fish hatchery). Its 406-mile journey begins beneath the granite spines of the Sawtooth Mountains in central Idaho, which are second only to the Tetons in their spectacular cragginess. Convoluted, the river then wraps through the Rocky Mountains for its

LEFT: *The Snake River cuts through Milner Gorge in an arid volcanic plain. This spectacular canyon lies amid the irrigated farmland of southern Idaho but is often dried up because of irrigation diversions.*

FAR LEFT ABOVE: *Lower Mesa Falls of the Henrys Fork forms one of the scenic centerpieces of the upper Snake River Basin.*

FAR LEFT BELOW: *As the Columbia's largest tributary, the Snake River begins with runoff from the backcountry of Yellowstone and Grand Teton National Parks. Heavy snows here on Mount Wister will melt and contribute to the river's flow throughout the summer.*

entire length. I once did a forty-three-day river trip there; the Salmon is the only river in America outside Alaska offering such an extended getaway.

Below the Salmon, the Grande Ronde River enters from Oregon after dropping from its headwaters in the Blue Mountains and flowing through spacious canyons shaded by ponderosa pine. At the industrial town of Lewiston, Idaho, the Clearwater River is the Snake's largest tributary by volume, with a watershed that marks a boundary between the drier forests to the south and the red cedar and fir to the north. Its Bitterroot Mountain headwaters fizz down through the incomparably pristine Selway River, whose road-accompanied twin, the Lochsa, joins to form the Middle Fork of the Clearwater.

Drained by the Salmon and Clearwater, ridge after ridge of pine and fir forest in central Idaho rank as America's finest remaining wilderness outside Alaska, with the most intact, undeveloped, unroaded acreage. Four million Idaho acres have been included in the National Wilderness Preservation System, much of it rocky, snowy high country. Twelve more million acres remained roadless but unprotected in the early 1990s, and timber sales on U.S. Forest Service land were planned with logging roads to be built into some of the wildest pockets of the Rockies. The Idaho Conservation League recommended 6 million acres for wilderness designation but continued to face a political stalemate.

From the mouth of the Clearwater to the Columbia, the Army Corps of Engineers built four back-to-back dams on the lower Snake so that grain could be shipped to foreign markets without using railroads. In 1976 the agency finished the uppermost dam. Another was proposed by utility companies at the Wild Mountain Sheep site in Hells Canyon, another was authorized above Lewiston at Asotin, and a whole series of dams was once considered for the Salmon River. But conservationists stopped the era of big dams in the Columbia Basin south of Canada at the Wild Mountain Sheep site, saving the best of what remains of Idaho's Snake and Salmon Rivers.

THE LOWER COLUMBIA

Below the mouth of the Snake, but still 324 miles upstream from the ocean, the Columbia in eastern Washington and then along the Oregon-Washington border is flooded back-to-back by McNary, John Day, The Dalles, and Bonneville Dams. Aiming due west toward the Pacific but still in a harsh and windy desert east of the Cascade Mountains, the Columbia receives the small Umatilla River of northeastern Oregon. Fighting a history of diversions and streamside abuse, the Umatilla Tribe and anglers have labored with encouraging success for the health of the stream; water has been returned to some reaches that had been dried up for irrigation.

Along the main stem Columbia at nearby Umatilla National Wildlife Refuge, I've stood spellbound at the flight of geese and ducks, whose numbers stretched from horizon to horizon. In one V formation after another, they flew over for hours in their autumn migration. Though seeing a mere fraction of the birds' original numbers, I was reminded of a journal entry written by William Clark while he camped along the Columbia: "I slept but very little last night for the noise kept up during the whole of the night by the swans, geese, white and gray brant ducks, etc. . . . they were immensely numerous, and their noise horrid."

West of Umatilla, the John Day River of central Oregon remains one of the longest, mostly undammed rivers in the greater Northwest, running for 243 undammed miles from ponderosa pine forests of the Blue Mountains to the backwaters of The Dalles Dam. This river still supports one of only a few salmon populations in the Columbia Basin unaffected by hatchery fish. At a four-mile-long preserve on the Middle Fork of the John Day, The Nature Conservancy aims to restore meandering channels and streamside growth of native plants—critical steps to reinstating salmon habitat.

The Deschutes River, just west of the John Day, also flows north to the Columbia, beginning its life on the lava-paved east slope of the Cascades, picking up steady heads of springwater and seasonal bursts of snowmelt, and curving through the central Oregon town of Bend. Several dams have blocked the once abundant runs of salmon, steelhead, cutthroat and rainbow trout, Dolly Varden, and kokanee, but below the dams the river rips over falls, boils through rapids, and hustles into a sharp-rock desert canyon. One of Oregon's most popular whitewater reaches extends from Sherar's Falls to the Columbia's backwater behind The Dalles Dam. The Oregon Trail veered away from the Columbia here at the head of an eight-mile-long rapid called The Dalles; pioneers either climbed south and skirted the slopes of Mount Hood or embarked on a sometimes terrorizing river trip aboard log rafts.

With a flow now greater than the Mississippi above its confluence with the Ohio River, the Columbia's 188,600 cfs from seven states and one province are poised at the barrier of the Cascade Mountains, which rise to more than 11,000 feet on either side and lie on a north-south axis confronting the westbound river. In this primordial contest of invincible force versus immovable object, the water won as the Columbia transected the backbone of the Cascades midway. While volcanism piled those mountains up, the Great River kept pace, crosscutting its course to the ocean. In volume of water passing by, this is the largest gorge on the continent.

Perhaps the best symbol of the Gorge's beginning was Celilo Falls, twelve miles above today's site of The Dalles Dam and one of the greatest rapids on the river. At this twenty-two-foot drop, Indians stood on log platforms, precariously overhanging the whitewater, and caught salmon. With spears, nets, and gaff hooks to snag fish by the gills, they collected their winter's supply with plenty of extra for trade. Coastal tribes brought goods from the sea, those of the interior brought buffalo robes, and in festive village encampments the people of many nations bartered for what they needed. Along Interstate 84, a relocated Native village remains as a cluster of modest homes that may be the oldest continuously inhabited community on the continent. But Celilo Falls is gone, thirty feet deep under the slack water of The Dalles Dam.

Anyone who drives through the Gorge experiences one of the most dramatically quick transformations of climate found in America. From east to west, the rabbitbrush desert of the Columbia Plateau becomes dotted by ponderosa pines and Oregon white oaks, then Douglas-firs on north-facing slopes, and then a water-world forest of aged western red cedars, western hemlocks, and Douglas-firs dripping in moss. Sunshine might

under seventy-five inches of rain.

Snowcapped Mount Adams, the third highest peak in the Cascade Range (Rainier and Shasta are higher), rises to 12,307 cloud-shrouded feet at the headwaters of the Klickitat River on the north side of the Columbia. This vivacious salmon and steelhead stream zips along for ninety-six miles—the longest completely free-flowing river in the lower Columbia region. Just west of the Klickitat, the White Salmon River also drops in chasms and waterfalls. Drawn by curiosity and the little river's perfect beauty, I've traveled up that valley, stopped to peer into its slippery canyons, then hiked to the headwaters on the snowy flank of Mount Adams, which rises like a white ramp to the sky. Because it enters the Columbia halfway through the Gorge, the White Salmon basin is a mixing ground for plant species from the arid east and rain-soaked west.

To the south, Mount Hood elegantly pierces the sky at 11,235 feet, a symbol of the Northwest with its permanent mantle of glaciers and snow-fields. These feed the White, Hood, and Sandy Rivers of Oregon. In this section of the Columbia, potent winds owe their origin to the desert lying eastward, where hot air rises and sucks in ocean air that whips upstream through the constriction of the Gorge. The steadiness of this air current has made the community of Hood River the wind surfing capital of the continent.

Dozens of small tributaries plunge over water-falls into the Columbia Gorge, its slopes blanketed by the mossy green of ferns, salal, and conifers. Here is a greater concentration of large waterfalls than anyplace else in the country but Yosemite Valley in California. Pitching in two tiers to the floor of the Gorge, 620-foot-high Multnomah

turn to a pelting rainstorm within ten minutes of driving time. In twenty miles, the Columbia takes us from a windblown desert with twelve inches of precipitation a year to misty rainforests soaked

Falls ranks as the fourth highest in the United States. Near the lower end of the Gorge, Bonneville Dam impounds the river one last time. Though still 146 miles from sea, the Columbia's gradient is exhausted, and high tides lap near the base of the dam.

While the Gorge's tributaries impress any visitor as showcases of nature, this corridor of the Columbia is packed full with Interstate 84, a two-lane highway on each side of the river, a railroad on each shore, dams with back-to-back flat-water floating barges, and a scratched sky of overhead powerlines snapping and crackling and dipping from one erector-set tower to another. But the Gorge is still one of a kind. To see the essence of the place, walkers can follow the steep trail up Beacon Rock, which juts 848 feet skyward as a Gibraltar-like plug of an old volcano at the north side of the river below Bonneville Dam. The Army Corps of Engineers once wanted to blast the rock to its root for use in building a jetty at the mouth of the river. The Biddle family, who owned the Beacon, fought and tried to give it to the state as a park. When Washington refused, Oregon offered to take the property, pressuring the state of Washington to finally accept the offer and preserve the landmark.

At the mouth of the Gorge, the pulp mill owned by the James River Company in Camas, Washington smokes the sky with rotten-egg odors, often smelled in Portland, and discharges 59 million gallons of wastewater daily, including dioxin, cyanide, copper, zinc, and formaldehyde, according to Northwest Environmental Advocates. Throughout the Columbia Basin, eleven of the nineteen pulp and paper mills discharged the cancer-causing dioxin in the 1990s. On the south side, the Sandy River offers blue-green depths of water accessible at two state parks only a half-hour's drive from Portland.

Dramatically different from the east side, the west slope of the Cascade Mountains in Oregon soaks up rain and snow and delivers them to the Columbia by way of the north-bound Willamette River and its colorful cast of tributaries. The Middle Fork Willamette sluices out of the mountains to the south, the McKenzie and Santiam systems flow from central zones, and the Clackamas drains the north. Though logged extensively, this western slope of the Cascades harbors isolated pockets of ancient forest such as those along the North Fork of the Middle Fork Willamette and Opal Creek above the Little North Santiam.

The McKenzie begins in Clear Lake, dammed by a lava flow 3,000 years ago, which flooded a forest whose stumps and broken remains can still be seen; though older than classical Greek ruins, the wood has nominally been preserved by frigid water. The Breitenbush River rushes past hot springs and into a dammed-up reach of the North Santiam. All the tributaries churn westward to the 37,400 cfs flow of the Willamette—the Columbia's third largest tributary.

The Willamette Valley accounts for some of the best of the Columbia watershed's 7.2 million acres of cultivated farmland. The river's main stem begins near Eugene and flows due north for 185 miles, undammed until almost at the tidal line. In this wide, temperate valley, so welcoming since the days of the Oregon Trail, 70 percent of Oregonians have settled, and these "west siders" account for about half the population of the entire Columbia Basin. The university towns of Eugene

LEFT: *One of dozens of waterfalls found in the Columbia River Gorge, this drop on Turner Creek plunges over lava ledges. Down below, the river has crosscut the Cascade Mountains, leaving side streams to plummet from alpine heights to sea level.*

Dwarfed by an ocean freighter, a runner enjoys a sandy beach near the mouth of the Willamette River.

and Corvallis and the state capital of Salem combine the ease of small-town life, the cultural buzz of cities, and the nearby open fields of farmland in front of mountain peaks, all of it strung together by the Willamette River, where a cottonwood corridor lines the banks.

To float logs and steamships, and to increase farming, the Willamette was channelized, its tapestry of wetlands drained, its sloughs and braids dried up and filled. More than half the river's winding distance in some sections was eliminated by shortcuts. Five channels in some reaches were consolidated into one. Farms and development soon blanketed the flats where floodwaters once spilled over in helpful ways that had lessened the flood crest downstream, deposited rich soils on the fields, revitalized groundwater, and nourished fish and wildlife in a bottomland forest corridor

up to six miles wide—a biological masterpiece of the West whose closest replication is now the Columbia's uppermost mileage in British Columbia. Today's simplified Willamette of a single main-stem channel poses a far greater flood risk because high waters now run off immediately without the opportunity to spread out across the floodplain.

For all the losses, the handicapped river that remains is a fine asset compared to thirty years ago when paper mills and towns slopped raw waste directly into the Willamette. The river has been the fortunate object of a difficult cleanup and is one example of success in cutting the vilest waste from point sources—those that come from single industries or towns. But the job is far from done. Up to 74 percent of the squawfish in the Newberg Pool, immediately upstream of Portland where the city may someday have to tap an additional water supply, were deformed. Pulp mill effluent, agricultural runoff, and urban storm water are the culprits.

At Oregon City, the Willamette once poured over a forty-foot waterfall, among the first industrialized sites in the West. Today, what is left of the great cataract lies below a dam that arcs across the upper lip of the falls, leaving only a residual plunge of water over rocks. Below, the Willamette dissipates its energy through a canyon of brick and smokestack industries rising from both shores in the style of an old New England mill town. The waters swirl into the tidal zone at Portland.

The sixth largest city on the Pacific Coast of North America, Portland and its urban area house over 1.7 million people. Here the broad, tidal Willamette splits the metropolis in half, a bustling downtown of interesting architecture to the west, a host of vibrant and livable neighborhoods to the east. An urban park named for Governor Tom McCall, who championed cleanup of the river, lines the Willamette, followed by docks and shipyards for ocean freighters and tankers. You would think the city was named for its busy port, but the fledgling settlement was in fact named by the toss of a coin, when a settler homesick for Portland, Maine, won out over one from Boston.

The "City of Roses" blooms with flowers in the spring and summer and is one of the more progressive cities in America for environmental protection, with 7,000 acres of parks. Residents delight in a magical view of Mount Hood, often hanging in the clouds as it is seen from hilltop neighborhoods. Reducing polluting car use, a downtown transit mall makes bus service easy, and city visionaries traded federal money for a new

freeway and built a light-rail system instead. The best urban energy plan in the nation, developed under Mayor Neil Goldschmidt in the early 1980s, called for efficiency improvements and energy savings of 30 percent.

Water quality still suffers from fifty-four sewers that overflow during rainstorms into the Willamette and the Columbia Slough, which lies in an eighteen-mile lowland along the river. The most contaminated waterway in the state, the Slough once made a wetland paradise for wildlife but now stagnates with 1.2 billion gallons of untreated sewage overflow a year. Sued by Northwest Environmental Advocates in 1991, the city has launched a $700 million program to fix the sewers by separating rainwater runoff from sewage lines.

With the added flow of the Willamette, the Columbia nears its end, but 102 miles of tidal channel remain, and the river still increases measurably in size. The Lewis River enters from the north after gathering waters from the south flank of Mount Saint Helens. The day after the Saint Helens eruption in 1980, the Toutle River, viscous with mudflows, ran at a temperature of ninety-two degrees—forty degrees more than normal. The most symmetrically cone-topped, snowy mountain in America was instantly decapitated when a cubic mile of earth blew sky-high into cinders, dust, and ash that spread noticeably over several states; trace deposits eventually encircled the globe. Saint Helens remains a volcanic specimen, a geologic laboratory, and a testament to the awesome power of nature; the mountain's summit gone, its north side scooped out, its forests leveled for miles by a pyroclastic blast of volcanic rock and hot air that exploded across the land and for miles flattened trees like toothpicks.

The Toutle River eventually enters the Cowlitz, whose headwaters drink in the Ohanapecosh River on the southeastern flank of Mount Rainier. Here is the Columbia Basin's ninth major national park, which features the Cascades' highest peak at 14,410 feet. Rainier also towers as the summit of the Columbia watershed, only eighty-four feet lower than California's Mount Whitney, the highest summit in the United States outside Alaska.

The four-mile-long Astoria Bridge spans the Columbia just a few miles before it reaches the Pacific.

Topped off with the Cowlitz, the Columbia now pushes west as an inland sea of one- to eight-mile width in tidal cycles that lap onto beaches where you can go running on the sand for miles. The river is so wide that explorer William Clark mistook it for the Pacific Ocean. The lower forty-six miles of estuary, where saltwater mixes with fresh, once supported an intricate belt of wetlands, but only 23 percent of the tidal swamps remain. Some Sitka spruce bogs still spread out in lowlands like water spilled onto a flat forest floor. At Blind Slough, east of Astoria, Oregon, an 800-acre Nature Conservancy preserve attracts bald eagles, otters, and salmon. The 35,000-acre Lewis and Clark National Wildlife Refuge consists of tidally flooded islands, vital to waterfowl.

The Great River of the West makes its final cut through the low hills of the Coast Range, which otherwise run nearly unbroken from San Francisco Bay to Puget Sound. Wintertime rains here can fall constantly, but this land at the latitude of Minnesota or southern Maine is surprisingly temperate, seldom freezing owing to the warm breath of the Japanese Current in the ocean.

Ten miles upstream from the river's mouth sits Astoria, occupied longer than any other American settlement west of the Rockies. Victorian homes and a downtown of intermingled commerce, residence, and industry rise on the hills. The waterfront sports cormorants and seals, hulking freighters on taut anchor chains, and rotting piers leading to abandoned, caved-in canneries from the heyday of commercial salmon harvest.

It's ironic that here on the lower Columbia, within a few days of their two-year goal of reaching the Pacific, Lewis and Clark had some of their most gripping difficulties. Soaking wet, they had to bivouac on the north shore, shelterless from rain and threatened by rising tides that swamped their boats and battered them with two-hundred-foot-long floating logs. On November 8, 1805, William Clark wrote, "The high hills jutting in so close and steep that we cannot retreat back, and the water of the river too salt to be used. Added to this, the waves are increasing to such a height that we cannot move from this place."

A river mouth of legendary hazard throughout history, the Columbia Bar has sunk about two thousand vessels and is considered the third most perilous river mouth on earth. About a dozen victims drown every year.

A jetty at the river's mouth was built by the Army Corps of Engineers from 1885 to 1917—it took that long to dump enough rock to boss the Columbia. The Corps ran a railroad line out into the ocean to construct a rock pile as wide as a football field and five stories deep. It extends into the sea for a remarkable seven miles on the south side, funneling the Columbia's currents and deterring the formation and unpredictable migration of sand bars. During low tide—and respecting the tides' schedule is utterly essential for safety—I've walked out on the jetty. Feeling both thrilled and threatened, I stood on that rock pile *in* the ocean, the endless Pacific tossing whitecaps in a fury to my left and the Columbia pushing with the accumulated force of each and every tributary on my right. A shorter jetty jags out from the north shore, where Cape Disappointment rises as a wave-pounded, rocky headland above a stormy Pacific.

Waters that have fallen as snow in Jackson, Twisp, or Invermere now mix with salty waves, and the fruit of runoff and nutrients from all of the watershed drifts out into ocean currents that run either south to California or north to Alaska. From the ocean, evaporation produces clouds that will bring next year's rain and snow to the mountains; the cycle is never-ending.

Even here, at the final flow of the Columbia,

the river reflects the heavy hand of people who have transformed this waterway from a golf course at its source to a channelized behemoth at sea-level jetties. Sandbars no longer congest the mouth because they are dredged away by the Army Corps of Engineers. The river rarely floods anymore. The rapids are gone. The salmon are nearly gone. Hanford's nuclear waste might pollute the water for millennia.

Meanwhile, people still emigrate to the region by the tens of thousands. People at one time were pulled by economic forces, but now they are pushed by the repellent of overurbanization in other regions, which raises housing costs, steepens taxes, increases crime, and aggravates a host of problems from water shortages to gang graffiti on the garage door. The ripples are felt throughout, as the Columbia Basin is bound by tendons and ligaments connecting economic systems to ecosystems.

From its source at a golf course to its end at this rock jetty built by the Army Corps of Engineers, the Columbia has been altered for commerce, yet extraordinary natural assets remain.

CHAPTER TWO

THE LONG SWIM HOME

THE RIVER AND THE FISH

Even three hundred miles offshore, salmon and steelhead can detect their river by its scent. The sleek, hearty fish have lived for several years at sea, but now they approach the mouth of the great waterway and, underneath its maelstrom of battling tide and current, they pass over Columbia Bar at Cape Disappointment.

They are bound upriver, for home. After entering freshwater, the salmon don't eat; instead, they consume body oil on their epic journey to come. Ascending the river's girthy trunk, some fish veer off at the Willamette, Deschutes, and John Day, but most plunge onward. They fin their way up the Snake River to the Salmon River, and on to its headwaters, some fish clocking nine hundred miles upstream from the Columbia's mouth. It's difficult to appreciate the challenge of swimming up one rapid, let alone surmounting hundreds of miles of opposing current. But the fish do it, up to thirty miles a day, propelled by the urge to reproduce, by the will to live, and

LEFT: *Bonneville is the first dam that salmon and steelhead encounter in their spawning run up the Columbia. The fish must surmount eight major dams in order to return to the Salmon River.*

even more, by the instinct that a whole species must live.

Chamberlain Creek is typical of many streams where the fish are headed. A tributary to the Salmon River, it arises in the pine woods and flowered meadows of the Rockies where wildness is the defining term of existence. Twisting and turning in its upper basin, the stream's transparent water flows like a life force over beds of colored gravel, bringing oxygen to the well-washed spaces between shiny stones. Camping at places such as this for days on end, I watch for the sun to melt the morning frost, the light as it reflects on the water, the buildup of clouds and power of storms, the marten and elk in their silent search for food. And I watch for the annual return of the salmon.

The headwaters lie deep in the Frank Church River of No Return Wilderness, a rare, large block of undeveloped, unlogged land that serves as a spawning grounds for fish that need clean water and undiverted flows. Wilderness is not essential, but careless use of unprotected areas has whittled away at salmon and steelhead streams; until we restore lost qualities, places such as Chamberlain Creek remain vital refuges to the creatures that will carry on the gene pool for the future.

The salmon's sense of smell, miraculously acute, leads them back to this stream where they were born, to where the female, with motherly care, will prepare a nest of gravel called a redd. Then the pair will mate in the supreme, culminating instant of their lives, and they'll leave fertile eggs among the clean, water-washed stones so that new salmon will again go to sea and again return to spawn. Their purpose in life fulfilled, their bodies spent in the effort, the adult salmon finally

rest. For once they become still, and one last breath of water filters across their gills.

Life-giving even in death, the salmon carcasses release ocean-collected nutrients to less fertile headwater streams. Decaying bodies of the spawned-out fish—still teethy and fierce with determination—feed an abundance of other wildlife from eagles to ravens to bears. The salmon are a "keystone" species, meaning that many other creatures depend on them. Along one salmon stream, researchers saw twenty mammal and twenty-three bird species eating the fish. Biologists have found that up to 18 percent of the nitrogen in riverside plants along salmon streams came from rotting salmon; up to 35 percent of the carbon in riparian insects was recycled from spawned-out fish. Even in the ocean, killer whales depend on salmon for up to 90 percent of their diet, and could disappear if the fish go extinct. Without the salmon, a large part of the life system of the Columbia region would collapse.

Resident fish such as trout, which don't migrate to the ocean, could never multiply to the vast numbers once seen in the anadromous or seagoing salmon and steelhead; the greater nutrient garden of the ocean is essential for the semi-solid runs of fish that once crowded the streams of the Basin and provided a fundamental building block of an immense ecosystem, with humans benefiting at its top.

The fish that have returned as reliably as sunrise for thousands of years symbolize the Northwest. You see them in the art of native people and on T-shirts, neckties, sundresses, coffee mugs, and lamp shades. The salmon best illustrate the fact that the Columbia River watershed is one unified place. All that we do to the water and land affects the journeys and lives of these creatures, and it indicates our respect, or lack of it, for the greatest emblem of the Northwest.

Now, two hundred years after white people first set eyes on these masterworks of creation, we have killed off nearly all the fish to produce cheap hydroelectric power and to run barges. Industries benefiting from the system oppose changes that might jeopardize federal subsidies they receive. Salmon supporters argue to cut the damaging subsidies and in the process restore some small share of the natural conditions that once made the Columbia the greatest salmon river on earth.

The story of this juxtaposition of values is one of surprising twists and turns and subterfuge in which the real world is seldom what it seems to be. It is the classic story of the Columbia. The story of these fish, and the people who caused their demise, and the people who tried to save them—all this is the central story of life that will be told for the rest of time along the Great River.

Summarizing two hundred years of history, Ted Strong said, "In 1805 two white explorers on their way down the Columbia River passed by thousands of sockeye headed back to their spawning beds. By 1990 these people would multiply a million times over and the sockeye would become two." A Yakama Indian and director of the Columbia River Inter-Tribal Fish Commission, Ted Strong and thousands of other people work to restore the declining runs of fish.

The Essential Habitat

The Indians had ten thousand good years living off the salmon, but then the problems began in 1866 when unregulated commercial netting of

RIGHT: *Clean beds of gravel, such as these in the North Fork of the Flathead in Montana, are critical as spawning beds for many fish species. Poorly controlled logging, grazing, and land development have caused muddy flows, ruining spawning gravels in many streams.*

ABOVE: *After being run through irrigation ditches and across fields where it accumulates silt and pesticides harmful to river life agricultural wastewater is channeled into the Snake and other rivers. Better management can solve these problems.*

the fine-tasting fish escalated toward a take of 43 million pounds per year. With government regulations, the runs again stabilized in the 1930s, and commercial fishing was eclipsed by the ugly twins of habitat destruction and dams.

Leading the assault on spawning habitat, logging caused erosion of soil that mucked over the gravel beds needed by the fish. The stripped mountainsides caused higher runoff during floods and diminished flows during droughts, all of it deadly to salmon. Uncontrolled cattle grazing eroded stream banks and watersheds. Irrigation diverted water essential to fish, and young fry became trapped in unscreened ditches leading to hayfields. Biologists for the Pacific Rivers Council estimated that land abuse has cut spawning habitat

in half, and biologist Willa Nehlsen found that 90 percent of salmon stocks suffer some degree of habitat loss. The finest spawning areas were the lower-elevation, lower-gradient, meandering waters with gravel streambeds. These rivers fell almost entirely into private ownership, and salmon are confronted with an obstacle course of diversion dams, ditches, development, broken-down banks, eroded shorelines, channelization, and rock-walled riprap. Responsible landowners are doing what they can to correct those problems, but most low-elevation habitat remains a purgatory to the fish.

Salmon recovery requires restoration of spawning habitat in streams, which is especially promising in the lower-river tributaries where the fish have only a few dams to surmount. In the John Day River, for example, the four thousand salmon that now spawn may once have numbered several hundred thousand. To repopulate the river, scores of stream miles can be fixed by building fences to control cows, reducing diversions, reinstating old channels, and replanting banks; all of it would benefit other wildlife and even cattle.

While habitat problems lie in headwater streams, other problems await at the opposite end of the salmon and steelhead's range. Shifts in ocean currents in the 1990s stemming from the warm water phenomenon, El Niño, resulted in less mixing of deep water with surface water and a corresponding reduction of food available to salmon off the Northwest coast. But ocean fluctuations are only a problem because human activities have so reduced the fish populations, which previously withstood nature's variations for thousands of years. Tim Stearns of the Save Our Wild Salmon Coalition recognized the importance of ocean conditions but noted, "We can't *do* anything about the ocean. We *can* do something about the condition of our streams."

THE PIVOTAL PROBLEM OF DAMS

As bad as the problems at either end of the salmon's peregrinations might be, the largest single impediment is not at the headwaters or in the ocean, but in between. Dams, built for hydroelectric power and barge travel, make it difficult or impossible for the fish to swim up and down the rivers. One-third of the original Columbia Basin habitat for salmon is blocked entirely by dams such as Grand Coulee and Hells Canyon, which have no fish ladders to allow the salmon passage. All fourteen dams on the main-stem Columbia hinder steelhead and salmon and two of them barricade the fish entirely from the Basin up above. Four dams on the Snake River eliminate many fish and another eight dams block passage entirely on the once-productive middle river. Hundreds of dams have been built throughout the Columbia watershed. According to the Northwest Power Planning Council, dams are responsible for 95 percent of the human-caused losses of salmon and steelhead smolts and adults.

The dams were built to solve human problems and to fuel the economy, but we have done far more than that. We have dammed at any cost, with little question, and sometimes for little reason. When the Army Corps of Engineers plugged the Columbia with McNary Dam in 1954, the *Walla Walla Union-Bulletin* reported with typical boosterism that the dam "will harness the tremendous force of the river into new, construc-

tive uses." The only reference to salmon was a placating statement issued from the Corps that a fishery program would "insure protection of the fishing industry." The Corps knew better. As pointed out by Anthony Netboy and Keith Petersen, who have written thorough histories, biologists said that the dams would kill off the fish, and many people in 1946 had pushed for a moratorium to stop McNary Dam, The Dalles Dam, and especially the lower Snake River dams. But on a flimsy and deceptive promise to spare the fish, the projects were approved with the belief that we could have it all. Eventually people recognized what was being lost, and realized that the costs were too great, and so dam building on the large rivers was stopped in the 1970s. But the last binge of construction occurred with the four dams on the lower Snake.

The dams kill migrating fish by blocking them from ascending the rivers and forcing them into ladders that resemble broad, flooded stairways with 700 steps in all on the Columbia and Snake route to spawning grounds. Between 37 and 61 percent of the adult fish still die trying to ascend the battery of dams. For years, however, the impression was that the fish were okay. Even in 1994, school students visiting Bonneville Dam peered with fascination through a picture window as a few salmon swam up the ladder, and they wrote in the Corps' register, "Thanks for showing us the fish." They didn't know that the dam killed salmon rather than saved them.

The biggest problem at the dams occurs during the salmon's downstream journey. For boosters, builders, and all the common people who wanted to believe in what they were doing, it was easy to reason that the downriver migrants had

Salmon and steelhead by the millions once spawned in the Columbia's tributaries. Many of those runs of fish are now endangered or extinct.

gravity on their side. But the dams created monumental hazards as water swept the tender, baby fish into hydroelectric turbines. Screens can deflect fish away from the intakes, but not all the dams were so equipped. Where screens were built, such as at Lower Granite and Little Goose Dams, they collected only 50 to 70 percent of the smolts. Many fish miss the screens, while others slam into the screens and get battered through high velocity pipelines bypassing the dams. More smolts might survive if water and fish were spilled over the top of the dams rather than all the water being piped into the turbines. But less electricity is produced that way. Supersaturation of nitrogen—killing fish with all the eye-popping horror of the bends—used to mean sure death to fish flushed over the spillways. Redesign of the water's splash zone on all but Ice Harbor Dam has solved much of the nitrogen problem except during times of extremely high flow, and "spill" is now one of the techniques that can be used for saving fish.

A problem even greater than the dams may be the scarcely moving flat water of the associated reservoirs. Young smolts coming down from the Salmon River have 350 miles of reservoir to negotiate. The small fish don't swim downstream but rather drift near the shore and rely on the current to push them. But there is hardly any current left. A predam journey of seven days might now take two months—for the lucky fish that make it. Smolts stall out in the dead water where they are sitting prey to northern squawfish, which, similar to Norway rats and cockroaches, enjoy a habitat advantage created by people. Meanwhile, each salmon's biological clock is ticking; thousands of years of genetics have programmed the salmon's physiology for "smoltification" from a freshwater

to saltwater species. But now the fish don't make it to the ocean in time. After construction of the Snake River dams, the death rate of downriver smolts jumped from an estimated 5 to as high as 95 percent. Recent tests may indicate a somewhat lower percentage, but the cumulative effect of the dams is still deadly and overwhelming to the surviving populations.

Not all the Columbia River salmon face imminent extinction. Several runs that do not go up the Snake River but stay in the main-stem Columbia remain less threatened. A stock of chinook called upriver brights—the largest naturally spawning run of fall chinook remaining in the lower forty-eight states—reproduce in America's only free-flowing section of the Columbia, at Hanford. Additional runs of salmon can ascend the middle Columbia dams without extreme difficulty because the dams are not very high. They can descend the main stem with some degree of success because a lot of water flows down the river. For now, relatively strong stocks go home to the Wenatchee River, and sockeye or red salmon return to lakes of the Wenatchee and Okanogan. The Snake River runs, however, once outnumbered them all.

Upriver dams for storage of irrigation water on the Snake hold back critical springtime flows, and the lower Snake River dams are difficult to pass. Confronted by the dual hazards of low flow and high dams, Snake River salmon have become a focus of concern—perhaps the most concern ever given to a species on the death row of extinction.

In a classic example of hubris from the dam-building era of 1930–1980, many people thought it was no problem to kill off the natural runs of fish. We could make our *own* fish. With artificially hatched salmon, at least the fish markets could stay in business. Thus, for forty years the "great concrete hope" of hatcheries allowed the Corps and hydropower developers to build more dams and kill more fish but supposedly mitigate the losses—a great fiction in retrospect. People were easily fooled because, by rearing young salmon in a protected environment, a higher percentage of fry do survive. But hatchery fish are not wild fish; they lack both the instincts and genetics that natural runs of salmon depend upon. Wild salmon have nine times better chances of surviving than hatchery fish. Yet, by competition and the gleaning of native salmon eggs to seed hatchery stocks, hatcheries diminish wild fish. Worse, roughly a hundred Columbia Basin hatcheries introduce diseases that thrive in crowded feedlot conditions and then spread outside them, infecting wild fish. Furthermore, interbreeding of hatchery fish with wild fish can narrow the gene pool; hatchery survival selects for fish best suited for a hatchery, not a wild environment. Biologist Nehlsen estimated that hatchery stocks harm half the remaining wild fish. To do this is not cheap; Columbia River hatcheries cost $537 million from 1981 to 1991, according to the General Accounting Office.

Worst of all, the government programs that dumped millions of pellet-fed offspring into the river for half a century masked the inexorable decline of wild, naturally spawning stocks so that many people remained unaware of the impending extinction crisis. The masking permitted commercial fishermen to continue their harvest, though they snagged wild fish perilously close to extinction in the same nets as the hatchery fish and sent them all to the same canneries. Lower Columbia River tribes believe that hatcheries are essential for a harvestable population of salmon, and they might be right, but in the 1990s many scientists argued that hatcheries were more of a problem than a solution. Historic Columbia Basin runs of 10–16 million fish—every one of them wild—were reduced to 0.3 million in 1995, and 80 percent of them were "stockies" from hatcheries.

SEARCHING FOR SOLUTIONS

To synthesize this array of difficulties stemming from the Depression Era notion that a big river could spin hydroelectric turbines for free, the Northwest Power Planning Council was formed by the U.S. Congress in 1980 with representatives appointed by the governors of Oregon, Washington, Idaho, and Montana. Congress charged the agency with planning for power needs, then added the responsibility of planning for restoration of salmon and steelhead by "equitable treatment" of fish and hydropower. Under this law, the mandated

By ascending the fish ladder at Bonneville, some salmon and steelhead navigate around the dam and continue their journey to their spawning grounds. The more difficult problem is getting the next generation of young fish past the dams during the downstream run.

restoration of runs that had been degraded because of hydropower was a far loftier goal than that of the Endangered Species Act, whose application would come later as a last-ditch effort following failures of the Power Planning Council.

The Council brought sensible oversight to power issues, in contrast to earlier decisions that had resulted in an economically disastrous decision to build nuclear power plants. Pursuing energy efficiency in the 1980s, the Council encouraged the conservation of 1,100 megawatts of electricity—enough for Seattle—with no new generation. In a spectacular, little-noticed success for conservation, the Council put 40,000 miles of critical streams off-limits to new impoundments. But lacking authority to direct the Army Corps of Engineers in its operation of the Columbia and Snake River dams, the Council labored without success to restore the anadromous runs. Though the law said power and fish were to be regarded as equals, cheap power was more abundant than ever and the fish were nearly all gone.

In the Columbia Basin, sixty-seven different stocks of salmon are already extinct. A "stock" or "run" is a genetically distinct population of salmon going up a particular stream, and while some mixing of runs occurs, each is essentially a separate species. Three major runs—all the Snake River salmon—have been added to the nation's endangered species list, requiring all reasonable efforts to avoid extinction. The Snake River coho were declared extinct in 1987, and another seventy-two runs are threatened but unlisted.

In 1981 the last cannery on the Columbia River had closed, ending the era of the Northwest's first great industry, one that over the years contributed vastly more in jobs and real value than the current barging and aluminum industries combined. Commercial fishing was potentially the most valuable and sustainable industry of all. But the fishermen have gone out of business or left for Alaska. With almost no fish left to catch, commercial harvest was altogether halted off the coasts of northern Oregon and Washington in 1994. The Institute for Fisheries Research estimated that 25,000 family-wage jobs have been lost in the region's fisheries since the Columbia dams were built. As recently as the 1970s, 5,000 sport and commercial boats could be seen at the mouth of the Columbia with 20,000 people fishing for salmon. Now there are none. The last statewide salmon season in Idaho—once a huge economic and sporting event—occurred in 1977.

By far the worst year to date, 1995 saw only 2,845 wild and stocked salmon of all kinds return to Idaho—6 percent of the ten-year average, which was already a pathetic ghost of the past. In 1961, for comparison, 93,300 wild chinook journeyed above Ice Harbor, where a dam soon blocked the lower Snake and its passageway to Idaho. Steelhead are likewise in big trouble. A 1995 appeal to the National Marine Fisheries Service (NMFS, commonly pronounced "nymphs") by conservation groups sought to list steelhead as endangered and documented that twenty-three runs in the Northwest were already extinct. In 1996, ten to fifteen remaining runs were found to be at risk by the agency. For now, stocked steelhead from hatcheries survive in catchable numbers in the Snake River basin. The current steelhead fishery is worth $90 million a year and 2,700 jobs, according to an economic study done for the Idaho Fish and Wildlife Federation.

A handful of agencies, dozens of organizations, and thousands of individuals have tried for more than twenty years to restore the lost vigor of the Columbia River salmon and steelhead. Science has proven the obvious: the fish need safe passage around the dams and faster travel time through the reservoirs.

Salmon smolts have drifted downriver for the millennia, but the Army Corps in the 1960s had the penultimate technovision for coping with the eight dams thrown up in the way: put the fish in trucks and barges and move them the same as we do wheat or wood chips. In this ironic perversion of transit whose logic might be questioned by the average second-grader, the wood chips now travel in the river and live fish go by truck or barge. This intensive management option sluices small, fragile smolts away from the uppermost dam and funnels them into a plumbed pipeline that water-slides down the slope of Lower Granite Dam, then dumps into a water-filled barge. When 400,000 fish are crammed aboard, a pilot fires up the diesel engines and drives the salmon and steelhead out to tidewater below Bonneville Dam. This solution avoids any compromise in the management of the river for hydropower, commercial barging, and irrigation. With determined persistence, the Corps operates the $52 million per year transit system for fish.

The Corps argues that more fish live through barging than would survive in the gauntlet of dams and reservoirs. The Corps assumes that bypass facilities and reservoir management will remain mostly unchanged. But state fish and wildlife agencies, tribes, and a coalition of forty conservation and fisheries groups called Save Our Wild Salmon all argue that the dams and manage-

ment must be improved, and that barging should be reduced or stopped. They maintain that even under the current system, more fish would survive without barging in wet years when water can be spilled over the dams without all of it flowing through the turbine death chambers. The fish supporters' chief display is a graph showing salmon and steelhead populations crashing since the 1970s when the Army Corps began barging every fish it could find. In fact, more fish returned when fewer were barged.

As the principal defense of barging, its proponents argue that, given the current condition of the dams and reservoirs, the fish might have gone extinct *sooner* without barging than they have with it. But even that statement is questioned. The Corps notes that most fish nominally survive the

At this fish-trapping facility alongside Lower Granite Dam on the Snake River, the Army Corps of Engineers funnels young salmon and steelhead into a barge for transport past the dams downstream. Many of the barged fish will never return.

things go wrong. In July 1994, at the worst possible time, the fish transport equipment malfunctioned and some 100,000 migrating smolts were killed. In 1996—a high water year with a rare chance to recover some lost ground—the Corps had intended to install a new bypass system at Lower Granite Dam by February but didn't begin the work until April, and soon had to force high water over the spillway. Once again, the mishap occurred at the worst conceivable time during the migration season; up to 70 percent of the migrating smolts suffered nitrogen gas trauma.

Though the natural river has become a Frankenstein, broken and grafted together almost beyond recognition, salmon advocates still believe that ecological solutions are necessary if the fish are to survive, and that to return the river to a more natural condition is the essential job. Charles Ray of Idaho Rivers United said, "Barging is a deadly dodge. It allows the federal agencies to remove the fish from the river instead of upholding their legal obligation to fix the river."

To tackle one of the most pressing repair jobs, Congress ordered the Corps to improve screening on the dams. The Corps and the Reagan/Bush administration Office of Management and Budget stalled until Senator Mark Hatfield of Oregon put a hold on Corps promotions to the rank of general. The improvements were ordered by Congress in 1987, but the final screen is scheduled for installment in 1998—eleven precious years later down the road toward extinction. So far, the screens are used solely to catch fish for barging and not to pass the salmon and steelhead safely downriver.

Beyond the improvements at the dams, the fish need an increased flow through the reservoirs

thirty-hour boat ride, but the agency fails to point out that few fish find their way back. Fragile wild fish may die of diseases spread in the crowded barges, and they respond poorly to the rough handling through pipelines, in water tanks, and on grates where they are tagged for tracking. And to flush them down faster, or they need *less* reservoir—a lower level of slack water to more closely approximate the flow of the old river. The American Fisheries Society—the professional organization of fisheries biologists—reviewed a formidable body of literature and reported, "Research supports that improved salmon survival is dependent on increasing river velocity and spilling water over the dams." The Northwest Power Planning Council went as far as Tennessee's Oak Ridge National Laboratory to find scientists who were not already involved in the Columbia River salmon issue to provide an unbiased opinion on the importance of water flow to salmon, and they reached the same, commonsense conclusions as did the American Fisheries Society. Since the mid-1980s, federal agencies tried to flush more water through the reservoirs with minimal success because water is held upriver for irrigation and hydropower, and also because the lower Snake reservoirs are so long that all the water upriver would not be enough. Something else needed to be done.

THE DRAWDOWN OPTION

Under Governor Cecil Andrus, the Idaho Department of Fish and Game and consulting engineers developed a plan in the early 1990s designed to solve the problem of Snake River salmon and steelhead with the least disruption to everyone. The levels of the four Snake River reservoirs would be lowered by about forty feet for two months a year—the window of time that steelhead and salmon need to float out to sea. Pat Ford, one of the most seasoned conservationists in the greater Northwest and a spokesman for Save

Our Wild Salmon, said, "The central appeal of the argument for drawdowns is that we'll be returning the river to a more natural state—to more like it used to be—and that will be beneficial to the fish." The Corps would have to modify the spillways and build new fish ladders on three of the four dams at a cost of $1.4 billion, according to Corps estimates (engineering consultants for the state of Idaho estimated the cost at $600 million). The one-time expenditure would be annualized at $100 million a year, according to Corps figures. That may sound like a lot of money, but the estimated value of lost salmon is $254 million to $507 million per year in personal income, reflected in 13,000 to 25,000 jobs, according to the Institute for Fisheries Resources in 1996. All told, $6.5 billion were lost in the commercial and sport fisheries and related economies because of the salmon decline.

Barge companies that ship mostly wheat from Lewiston, Idaho would be affected by the drawdown plan, as would fourteen irrigators that pump from the reservoirs, and hydroelectric users. But the barging would be interrupted for only two months in the spring, a period when only 5 percent of the wheat is shipped. Many other river navigation systems, as notable as the upper Mississippi, are routinely closed for two months a year due to ice. Cargo could be shipped by rail or truck, as all of it was until 1976. The drawdown proposal included payment to industries for the inconvenience and damages resulting from lowering the reservoirs—a $6.5 million per year cost that was expected to decline over time as the market adjusted to new schedules.

The irrigators' problem with drawdown could easily be fixed by government-financed extensions

LEFT ABOVE: *Adequate flows of water are essential for the health of fisheries and other stream life. Now rarely seen, this volume of 12,000 cubic feet per second at Shoshone Falls on the Snake was common before the river was dammed and diverted for irrigation.*

LEFT BELOW: *At the same spot, flows over Shoshone Falls are cut to a trickle. Natural high water in the spring and summer has been reduced to accommodate irrigation needs, drying up some sections. In the lower Snake River, healthy flows are critical for salmon and steelhead migration.*

of intake pipes farther into the reservoirs or clear to the river, for that matter, as the reservoir storage is not needed. Concerns over hydropower sound as though they would be a big issue but, in fact, firm power that can dependably be sold from the four dams would be reduced by only 25 average megawatts according to Power Planning Council data and would have a negligible effect on the Columbia hydrosytem. One reason for the low figure is that the reservoirs would be drawn down in late spring when demand for power is low in both the Northwest and California. The power being given up for the fish simply isn't worth much economically, and is easily replaced at that time of year. Some nonfirm or surplus power being sold to California would be lost, but it has minimum economic value because its supply cannot be guaranteed, with or without the drawdown. Considering all the effects of drawdown, a less intrusive scenario for temporarily lowering reservoirs and ameliorating the effects of dams can hardly be imagined.

Knowing that the salmon and steelhead's time was running out, as was his fourth term in the governor's office, Cecil Andrus pushed his plan hard with the Northwest Power Planning Council, which after litigation against them, endorsed drawdowns in 1994. The National Marine Fisheries Service meanwhile wrote a separate plan as required by the Endangered Species Act. NMFS proposed new fishing limitations, revision of hatchery programs, habitat improvement in tributaries, and increased flow over the dams. But with political pressure from Democratic House Speaker Tom Foley of eastern Washington, whose goal was to keep Kaiser Aluminum in Spokane and to satisfy his irrigation constituents, NMFS failed to rec-

ommend drawdown of the Snake River dams. The Idaho Department of Fish and Game filed a lawsuit, and U.S. District Judge Malcolm Marsh issued a scathing ruling: "Instead of looking for what *can* be done to protect the species from jeopardy, NMFS and the action agencies have narrowly focused their attention on what the establishment is capable of handling with minimal disruption." In 1995 NMFS produced a draft recovery plan for endangered salmon and recommended drawing down John Day Reservoir on the lower Columbia in 1996 if money were available. It wasn't. Other drawdowns in this lackadaisical schedule are to be decided upon in 1999.

In what might appear to be a front of budding consensus, the Northwest Power Planning Council plan, the NMFS draft, and the Inter-Tribal Fish Commission plan all called for a mix of habitat improvement, spill of water over the dams in critical times, and drawdown of at least some reservoirs. But the combined weight of their arguments didn't for a minute mean that the agencies controlling the dams, much less the political heavyweights behind the scenes, would agree.

The Bonneville Power Administration (BPA) —a federal Department of Energy agency that markets the power from the federal dams in the Columbia Basin—resisted the drawdown proposal with the grip of a bureaucracy fearing for its life. Without even studying the issue, BPA announced that power prices would skyrocket. This false, ultimately embarrassing claim was later dropped for a second line of defense: nobody can "prove" that the drawdown would be effective. "More study" was needed. Though BPA had opposed a drawdown test, chief administrator Randy Hardy in 1995 explained, "We need a way to demonstrate that the drawdown will work. We need to know what the problems really are. The salmon are in trouble across the board—here, in British Columbia, and in the coastal streams. It's not just the Columbia River dams." The Corps, which was in direct charge of operating the dams, also fought the drawdown proposal and, without researching the real cost, threw out an estimate of $4 billion, which was later reduced to nearly one-fourth that amount. Forced to recognize the logic of the Northwest Power Planning Council's plan, but still resisting it, the Corps agreed to a tentative schedule of drawdown testing over a period of years.

Even with this resistance, it seemed that there was hope. It seemed that eventually the dams would be modified and the reservoirs drawn down. But then Cecil Andrus' final term expired. Republican farmer Phil Batt won the next election and promptly abandoned the drawdown plan, saying that it was "very injurious to other parts of the economy." He vowed "not one drop" of Snake River water for salmon. With Idaho and Montana in opposition and Oregon and Washington in favor of drawdowns, the Planning Council lay deadlocked. Lacking a clear mandate, the hard-earned drawdown plan languished. In 1995 Council director Ed Sheets recognized, "When two senators and the governor of Idaho oppose the plan, you have a problem." Batt's administration eventually proposed to barge fewer fish and agreed to release upper Basin water, provided Idaho farmers didn't "need" it, but he refused to reopen the drawdown question because of objections from the port city of Lewiston and because of upriver farmers' fear that any change regarding water is bad change. While the salmon need a less-dammed environment to migrate through with less reliance on barging, Batt's plan promised only the latter, a painless step for the Governor to take but one that may make little sense unless preparations are made for the smolts to be sent through the reservoirs and over the dams.

The industries were delighted, not only with the drawdown proponents' misfortune on election day in 1994 but also with the report of a supposedly independent panel. Under the auspices of the National Research Council, a group of scientists in 1995 reported that major changes in salmon strategy were needed, such as improved management of hatcheries and reduced harvest of wild fish. It did not recommend drawdown because of its cost and the lack of proven effectiveness. The cost was arguably an issue for politicians, not scientists, to consider. The report endorsed the Corps' barging operations and in the jargon of painstaking academic caution stated, "No investigator to date has provided the Columbia River region with experimental results that demonstrate higher survival of inriver migrants than transported migrants at any discharge level." The Research Council indicated that a different conclusion may be in order after "such experimental data become available." Ironically, the barging option had never been exposed to the "proof of benefit" standard.

Responding to the panel's report, Tim Stearns of Save Our Wild Salmon said, "Scientists often prefer to focus on uncertainties," and he argued that without trying, there will never be proof of effectiveness. "We *know* the fish are going extinct under the barging option."

"Supporters of the status quo say that if you can't *prove* something will benefit the fish, then don't do it," reflected Angus Duncan, an energy specialist who became chairman of the Northwest Power Planning Council. "But we will have to learn to cope with uncertainty and not be paralyzed by it. Why, in applying the 'best science available,' shouldn't we give the benefit of the doubt to restoring some measure of historical, pre-European settlement conditions, knowing that salmon thrived under those?" His answer: "Because the science is being stood on its head and bent around corners to protect the status quo and those with big financial stakes in it."

One hydropower expert sat on the Research Council's panel: Don Chapman, who has earned a very good living for more than a decade working under contracts for the hydroelectric industry. For this report about the biology of fish, the team excluded biologists from the fishery agencies, tribes, and environmental groups. The Research Council used a computer model paid for by BPA and the Columbia River Alliance—an industrial group—when other models were available from the Northwest Power Planning Council and the Inter-Tribal Fish Commission. Referring to the scientists on the payroll of the industries, Ted Strong said, "Science has become a commodity rather than a standard. The money that precedes science has bought science."

Criticizing not only the Research Council's panel but also a Snake River Salmon Recovery Team convened by NMFS, ex-governor Cecil Andrus bluntly stated, "In my opinion, some of those scientists were bought and paid for by BPA and the industries. Why do you think BPA keeps hiring them? Good science comes from a group of individuals who have no financial interest in the questions." The Recovery Team's energy spe-

cialist sat on the panel and then went to work for the aluminum and utility companies.

Pat Ford criticized the panels for asking the wrong question. "They asked if barging the fish is better than sending them through the reservoirs in the existing system. They didn't inquire much about the likelihood of improvement by changing the system. The tribal biologists, on the other hand, asked, 'Will we ever restore the runs with barging?' The answer was clearly, 'no.'"

With hired scientists, public relations, and political pressure, the industries, BPA, and the Corps stonewalled the Andrus plan. Their new reason: scientists were not in agreement that the drawdown would work. Yet if the biologists working for the industries and hydropower agencies were taken out of the picture, there appeared to be widespread agreement that drawdown was important. In 1996, the Independent Scientific Group reported to the Northwest Power Planning Council and corroborated that drawdown or draining of at least some of the reservoirs was vital, not only to the fish's migrating speed but also to the food chain in the reservoirs—critical to the migrating smolts. Addressing the issue more thoroughly than any previous scientific group, the panel had been convened by the new Power Planning Council representatives because they felt the Council's 1994 plan went too far. The scientists reported rather that the plan had not gone far enough. Angus Duncan said, "My hope is that the Planning Council's 1994 recommendations including drawdowns will become the status quo in planning—that it will have to be disproved or implemented. With that plan on the books, eventually the opportunity will open to do something effective."

BPA and the Fish

As if the fate of the perpetrator were tied to the fate of the victim, the BPA also fell on hard times when the fish crashed toward oblivion. Controlling the largest bloc of power in the West and providing 50 percent of the electricity in the Northwest, the agency had enjoyed half a century of smooth sailing in deluxe headquarters, the ability to offer electricity at bargain rates to wholesalers, and a staff so large that the public affairs director could refer me to one of several media specialists.

The easy times ended with the nuclear power debacle of the Washington Public Power Supply System (WPPSS). Based on overestimated growth, underestimated construction costs, blind boosterism of utilities, and a systematic rejection of cautionary advice regarding nuclear power, the BPA under Donald Hodel in the 1970s had bought into not one but five nuclear construction projects. Hodel accused those recommending caution as "the anti-producers, the anti-achievers. The doctrine they preach is that of scarcity and self-denial." He accused his opponents of wanting to "bring this region to its knees." But Hodel is the man who brought real meaning to that phrase. One nuclear plant was built and the others canceled after the largest bond default in American history. To relieve individual investors—in effect transferring the burden of error from them to BPA ratepayers—the agency saddled itself with $7 billion of debt. For the aborted plants, Northwesterners now pay an extra $3.75 to $10 on the typical $50 monthly utility bill. BPA's nuclear debt for one year of nonoperating nuclear power plants in 1991 was $323 million.

In this unending economic nightmare for BPA ratepayers, the one nuclear plant that does operate *costs* more than it generates in power sold. Inefficient and plagued with problems, this reactor at the Hanford nuclear reservation has been cited by federal authorities many times for safety and other violations. Closing it would save BPA ratepayers $60 million a year.

Even with the drag of WPPSS debt and sharp increases in wholesale rates, BPA power still sold for only 60 percent of the average nationwide. Industrial rates were much less, and it was hard to think of the agency as anything but a gravy train built under federal financing and selling an unquestionably needed product to a completely captive market. Then a seemingly unrelated push for efficient jet aircraft led to development of turbine engines powered by natural gas, which in turn powered electric generators used by industries. At the same time, natural gas production increased in the West and Canada. Then, in 1992, Congress began deregulating the wholesale utility industry, opening up BPA's market to the competition. Losing its monopoly was a bitter pill for BPA to swallow, but Congress in 1995 also broadened the agency's authority to sell excess power outside the region. Economist Zach Willey of the Environmental Defense Fund reported that if BPA lost its cheapest wholesale customers it could more profitably sell the freed-up power to California and the Southwest.

Shackled by nearly $1 billion of annual costs to the nuclear power plants along with subsidies to big industries, BPA also needed to fund the mitigation of salmon losses owing to the hydrodams. After natural gas suppliers offered tempting contracts to some industries, BPA lost about 700 megawatts' worth of sales, putting officials into a

The upper reaches of the Salmon River provide excellent spawning grounds for salmon that manage to navigate the passage around the dams.

panic—real, paranoid, or contrived—that wholesale customers in significant numbers would abandon the BPA ship.

Talk grew of disbanding the agency altogether, of splitting off its grid of powerlines from the infrastructure of dams and, in a mode fashionable during the Republican Congress of the mid-1990s, privatizing whatever utilities wanted to buy. Some feared insider deals would transfer BPA's public wealth to private hands and sever the residual New Deal ties of social obligation, such as responsibility for the fish that the power system kills.

Meanwhile, the fluctuations in demand kept everybody off balance. A projected deficit in the 1970s had given way to a surplus of power. By 1989, regional growth had brought another prospect of shortage, but that was suddenly transformed into the new power glut of 1995. All the time, both shortages and surpluses were referred to in slick doublespeak as reasons to slight the fish: shortages meant that electricity could not be sacrificed; surpluses meant that rates had to be lowered to keep BPA customers on board, with a resulting scarcity of funds to pay for salmon restoration. A bizarre juxtaposition of values resulted. Power was in such supply that industrial rates dipped lower. Aluminum companies paying one-third the national rate pointed to competing new smelters in Asia and threatened to abandon BPA, which complied by dropping rates again. But simultaneous efforts to quit diverting water through turbines in order to save fish provoked stubborn opposition because "valuable" electricity would be lost.

Facing competition and an accumulated burden of bills and debts, BPA's response was a curious one. It cut some staff and trimmed its fish and wildlife budget, but among all the other things it could have done, it chose to lobby Congress for an exemption from the Endangered Species Act, the Northwest Power Planning Act, and other fish and wildlife laws. On one hand, the agency had prided itself on spending money for the fish; in 1995 Assistant Administrator Jack Robertson said, "We've spent $5.5 billion for fish and wildlife enhancement, which may be more than in any other similar program in the world. We've *got* to save those fish." But if BPA got its exemption from the law, it could continue to pay its other bills and continue to provide big subsidies to industrial users without having to pay for increasing salmon recovery costs.

BPA's assault may have been the most serious attack on America's keystone environmental statute since its passage in 1973. If this federal agency didn't have to obey the law for endangered species as significant as salmon and steelhead, why would anybody? And BPA had just the man to push the exemption through: Republican Senator Slade Gorton of Washington, who proposed a blanket waiver from the Endangered Species Act

and other laws. But Gorton quickly encountered the Clinton administration, which warned that the Republican bill would be vetoed.

Gorton's approach was familiar to Inter-Tribal Chairman Ted Strong, accustomed to a history of assault on treaties with Native American nations from the Penobscots in Maine to the Quileute in Washington. "The U.S. government is struggling to keep its word. The Congress would rather change the law, so that the salmon are not protected, than force its citizenry—especially its corporate citizens—to pay for the cost of environmental degradation they have caused."

Democratic Senator Patty Murray of Washington jumped into the fray to avert wholesale loss of endangered species protection, pushing Republican Senator Mark Hatfield of Oregon to compromise and abandon the hard-line, gut-the-Act stance proposed by Gorton. A 1995 deal pushed through by Hatfield capped the average amount of BPA's fish expenses at $435 million per year for six years and made available $325 million in federal money for costs exceeding BPA's obligation. Beyond the agreed-upon prices, the fish could presumably be allowed to go extinct.

Pleased with the agreement getting his agency off the financial hook of escalating obligations, Randy Hardy said, "A limit on the budget will lead to better choices."

Others saw a hidden agenda of getting rid of the salmon once and for all. With the spending cap, implementing the drawdown was assumed to be impossible. Retired NMFS biologist Merritt Tuttle called the spending limit "the cap for the salmon's tomb." Ted Strong said, "This agreement is about saving the BPA from bankruptcy; it is not about saving the fish."

The salmon cap has drawn attention to a numbers game in which accountants may end up being more important than biologists in determining the fate of the fish. While BPA said it spent $350 million on salmon in 1994, only $86 million of that was direct payments for fish—money to hatcheries, studies, habitat projects, and the like. Of the remaining $270 million, most was not *spent* at all but rather was part of an accounting exercise reflecting the "foregone opportunity cost" of water that was passed over the dams for the fish instead of run through power plants. This accounting assumes that all the water in the river belongs to BPA and exists solely for hydropower; any water released for fish is a "cost." Few other businesses can claim that sales they didn't make—such as from closing shop on Sunday—constitute such a cost. You might as well assume that the river exists solely for fish, since they were there first, and that any water diverted for hydropower should be paid back for fish. But the salmon are assumed to be worthless on the accounting ledgers. The "foregone opportunity cost" is of course included in the $435 million price cap, allowing BPA to meet its impressive-sounding obligations while spending only $86 million or so.

If the "foregone opportunity cost" were not considered a real cost, then the price cap would include plenty of money for drawdown of the Snake River dams. For all its misleadings, the foregone cost is defensible in some economic theory—so long as the costs of other nonpower uses of water are also included and evaluated by comparable criteria on a level playing field. This qualification is well worth some investigation.

Science and economics indicate that we can solve the salmon's problems. The fish did relatively well until the lower Snake River dam complex was built. Yet in spite of old promises, big money, long-standing laws, public opinion, the Northwest Power Planning Act, the Endangered Species Act, Indian treaties, appealing rhetoric by everybody, and a general sense of outrage, it does not happen. Why not? What really drives this system of dams and reservoirs and power plants? Who really makes the important decisions?

INDUSTRIAL SCALE SUBSIDIES

A portrait of political influence comes into focus by looking at the industries that use the dams.

The direct subsidy to the irrigation industry that BPA serves totals well over $85 million per year, according to analysis by BPA and the Columbia River Basin Institute. Most of this sum comes from federal pumping of irrigation water, which is provided at cut rates to irrigators at a BPA ratepayer subsidy of $50-60 million per year. Some of this is for food on the table, but 70 percent of the river basin's water goes to low value crops such as hay, which can be grown throughout much of the U.S. More than 30 percent of the crops grown with the subsidized water are in chronic surplus; for those crops, the government, for many years, has paid cash subsidies so that farmers will curtail production. Nearly all water in the huge Columbia Basin Project of eastern Washington serves agribusiness giants such as Nestlé, Conagra, and J. R. Simplot—one of the wealthiest men in the West whose agricultural empire grows the potatoes that are rendered into McDonald's French fries. The industrial agriculture of the middle Columbia benefits one-sixth the number of farmers envisioned by New Deal planners, who had originally justified the subsidies to help family farmers through the Great Depression. The hollow justification has had adhesive staying power even amid the free-market rhetoric of the 1990s, aggressively expounded by the same interests that reap the subsidized largesse.

Beyond the pumping subsidy, the federal government paid for 97 percent of the construction costs of Grand Coulee Dam, one of the most subsidized irrigation projects in the country. This amounted to $2 million per 960-acre farm in the project area, according to Department of the Interior estimates in 1986. Farmers pay as low as two dollars per acre-foot for water that costs taxpayers and ratepayers fifty dollars to deliver.

A problem of inequity, typical in the West, is especially egregious here. The House Interior Committee in 1989 reported that the Columbia Basin Project will receive a water subsidy of $2.8 billion, amounting to $5,015 per irrigated acre, compared to $109 for the Minidoka Project of southern Idaho, and absolutely no water subsidy for the great majority of American farmers who compete to sell the same crops.

Irrigators Basinwide remove and do not return 14 million acre-feet a year from the rivers, according to the Northwest Power Planning Council. On top of the direct irrigation subsidies, this causes a loss of up to $350 million annually in foregone power revenues. These "costs" for irrigation are comparable to those for salmon, but BPA doesn't complain about irrigation losses, and the agency has not asked for a "cap" on those costs.

Then there are subsidies piled on top of subsidies. In the 1980s the irrigators of the Columbia River Basin Project began to take an additional 400,000 acre-feet per year in flows that the government pumps uphill from Grand Coulee Dam for almost free. The water is used to produce $10 million per year from new, small hydroelectric facilities built with tax-exempt financing. Irrigators sell this power for twenty-seven times the amount they pay the government for the electricity needed to deliver the same water to the irrigators' hydroelectric plants. Then they keep the profits. The added diversion for this clever enterprise takes water away from the river and from already existing public hydroelectric plants that would otherwise serve BPA's ratepayers.

Beyond the irrigation subsidies, there is the barging industry, which is even more thoroughly subsidized. The industry's take here includes $16 million per year to cover all barging-related construction of the dams and most of the cost of operating the locks. In addition to that, each time a lock is opened to let a boat through, 43 million gallons of water escape—enough to otherwise aid a lot of salmon on their downstream journey, or farm 50 acres all summer, or generate $700 worth of electricity and supply a Northwestern home for a year. The locks of the Columbia-Snake River system are opened 16,000 times a year, at a hydropower cost of $11 million. While the BPA charges water released for salmon as a "cost" to its program, it does no accounting for this water released at the locks.

Taxpayers from towns where the ports are located also subsidize barging. Lewiston and Nez Perce County residents alone paid an extra $487,000 in 1992 to keep their port alive, a local tax to make this small city in the Rocky Mountains a seaport, 465 miles from the ocean and already well served by rail. Without these gifts of taxpayers and ratepayers, rail service from Lewiston would be cheaper than barging, as pointed out in studies by economist Philip Lansing and others. The principal commodity in this swap of salmon for fully subsidized barging is wheat going to Asia.

All these figures are a realistic indication of how much money the Northwestern rate payers and U.S. taxpayers are spending in subsidy programs that inadvertently drive the salmon toward extinction.

More than irrigation and barging, the Northwestern aluminum industry, which produces 43 percent of America's aluminum, is the really big user of hydroelectricity. Kaiser, ALCOA, and Reynolds moved to the Columbia because of cheap power. The industry uses 20 to 33 percent of BPA's electricity. This equals the entire yield of six-and-a-half of the eight dams on the Snake-Columbia system. The industry pays 2 cents per kilowatt hour, compared to 4.6 cents paid by BPA's residential users.

The industry's subsidy from BPA ratepayers is $180 million a year, according to Jim Lazar, an economics consultant working for government agencies and utility companies. This comes to $25,000 per year for each job in the Northwest's aluminum plants. Aluminum industry jobs totaled 7,000 in 1995, compared to 62,000 that had depended on salmon and related industries in the Northwest before 1989 and contributed $1.25 billion to the region's economy with scarcely any subsidies at all, according to data collected by the Pacific Rivers Council. The aluminum jobs totaled 0.2 percent of the Northwest's labor pool in 1995. Annual new job creation in the

Northwest in the mid-1990s, for comparison, was 2 to 2.5 percent; if the aluminum industry left tomorrow, the job losses would be absorbed in one month.

Even with the aluminum corporations' cut-rate power, many analysts and insiders speculate that the industry may abandon the area within twenty years, but not until cheap power for their short tenure in the Northwest has served as a principal justification for driving the salmon to extinction. A conservation and taxpayer coalition maintains that requiring the aluminum industry or its replacement customers to pay market value for the power could save BPA $214 million a year.

One reason BPA charges such low rates to the aluminum industry is that the smelters consume electricity steadily, year-round, which means predictability. But a bigger reason is political influence. The aluminum companies, not counting affiliated individuals, gave $16,000 to Slade Gorton's campaigns through 1995. In negotiating for new contracts that year, the industry was a principal supporter of the BPA price cap on salmon restoration, without which power rates could conceivably go up. Aluminum producers also talked BPA out of charging them for any share of the agency's debt resulting from the nuclear power fiasco of WPPSS, leaving the region's ratepayers holding that $7 billion bag even though the decision to build the nuclear plants was made with aluminum industry support.

When the BPA agreed to new contracts with the aluminum companies in 1995 at a 15 percent reduction from their already-bargain-basement rates, Clinton administration Energy Secretary Hazel O'Leary halted the back-room, sweetheart deal. Senator Hatfield quickly summoned the secretary to a hearing room at the Capitol. Flanked by five other Northwestern senators fond of free-market rhetoric when speaking in more-public forums, Hatfield cut off O'Leary's explanations and with stony authority awaited her compliance. The new contracts were approved.

Regarding the various subsidies to power users, BPA administrator Randy Hardy said, "We're eliminating most of the subsidies that we can administratively eliminate. The rest will require legislation." Yet few subsidies were cut and the costs for salmon were the only ones to be officially "capped." The BPA's big legislative initiative was not to cut aid to special interests but to get exemption from the Endangered Species Act. The agency's costs went up and residential rates charged to Puget Power, Portland General Electric, and Pacific Power and Light went up, but the rates to the aluminum industry went down even further.

Electric utilities serving homeowners and businesses with Columbia hydropower are also adamant in their resistance to change. As a result of low electricity rates, per capita consumption is 61 percent above the national norm. Residential increases needed to pay for salmon restoration might raise rates 6 percent, but a 47 percent increase in rates would be necessary just to reach the national average.

The BPA's recent annual figure of $86 million spent on fish plus $228 million in foregone power sales in 1994 sounds like a lot of money, but compared to what? The WPPSS debt on dead nuclear plants is $323 million a year, and the one nuclear plant that operates costs up to $60 million more annually. The irrigation subsidy is about $435 million a year counting foregone power costs. The navigation subsidy is about $25 million a year while almost nothing is paid by the barging companies. The aluminum industry gets a price break of $180 million or more a year. *River of Red Ink,* a report by taxpayer and conservation groups, documented nearly $500 million annually in salmon-killing subsidies that taxpayers and ratepayers deliver to industries of the Northwest.

The subsidies were compassionately begun during the Great Depression, but since then they've grown to serve not poor people but wealthy individuals, not new industries but powerful multinational corporations, not socially justified principles but the most blatant of profit motives.

MAXIMIZING POLITICAL INFLUENCE

Playing political hardball, the irrigators, bargers, and aluminum producers have joined forces in an organization called the Columbia River Alliance for Fish, Commerce, and Communities. Director Bruce Lovelin said in an interview that his group "calls for salmon restoration in a way that does not reduce the viability of industry and commerce on the river." He called the Columbia River "a $30 billion economic driver to the Northwest" and claimed that "when we defend the dams, it gives the public the impression we're in denial. But we need to look at habitat, hatcheries, and harvest. People say we're trying to divert attention away from the dams, but we don't want to end up helping salmon in only one part of their life cycle."

The Alliance director's defense of the taxpayer and ratepayer giveaways was that the irrigation subsidies are "fixed in statute." Regarding barging, he said, "The navigation industry pays a tax on fuel." The tax, in fact, is ten cents per gallon and goes to new construction, not to operation and maintenance and certainly not to foregone power sales. All the accumulated fuel taxes on the entire Columbia River system since the tax began were enough to pay for only half the cost of new locks recently built at Bonneville Dam, which cost taxpayers another $170 million over and above all the other barging subsidies. Lovelin maintained that the aluminum industry is not subsidized at all, that it simply negotiated good contracts for power. To its credit, according to Lovelin, "they have avoided involvement in the WPPSS debt." He complained of a well-financed effort by environmentalists against the Alliance but refused to disclose the budget of his organization, which is supported by all the involved industries.

The influence of the Columbia River Alliance is what prevents reform of the system from occurring. As Pat Ford said, "The industries are afraid of losing their subsidies and scared of having to pay for changes to the system."

"The Alliance was everyplace we were, pushing their view," said Merritt Tuttle shortly after he retired from the National Marine Fisheries Service where he served as division chief in Portland. "They had a huge media campaign going on every day. I constantly got calls from reporters asking me to respond to what they'd just heard from the Alliance—always different from what the fishery agencies and tribes were saying. There's not one fishery agency or tribe that believes what the Alliance says. I think there's a deliberate attempt to drive the fish to extinction."

Tuttle continued with twenty years of reflection on the pressures that consumed his career much as they consumed the fish that he worked to save. "As the fisheries problem became known, two broad fronts emerged from the bowels of industry. One was to gut the Endangered Species Act. The other was to renege on the promises made to fishing interests before construction of the dams. Reneging would be easy—just place a cap on salmon costs. Corporate welfare is protected but everything else is up for grabs. Instead, why not use that money to bring back the fish?" The fish, Tuttle pointed out, were public property that we all once had for free.

The political leverage of the Alliance sustains policies that have "communized the costs and privatized the profits," as biologist Ed Chaney stated.

A reincarnation of the Alliance in 1996 had the curious title of Northwesterners for More Fish. Senator Slade Gorton's name greeted readers at the top of the attendee list for the founding meeting on February 16, 1996, held at an exclusive club in Spokane. The industry-backed group proposed to spend $2.6 million on public information in its first year of effort to rescind endangered species protection for Columbia River salmon. According to the group's prospectus, it was affiliated with Project Common Sense, which was "set up to create awareness of excessive government regulation in health care and various environment issues including the Endangered Species Act." This who's who of resource industries in the Northwest planned to hire Washington, D. C. ad men from Republican political campaigns to sell their extinction message as something that was good for fish. Presumably they were talking about suckers and carp, which survive in the warm flat water of the reservoirs. The prospectus recognized the need for "exposure during the upcoming presidential and congressional elections" and for presentation "in a way that invokes passion from the public." This thinly veiled invitation made clear that donations to the group could be a clever way for industries to contribute additional money benefiting their favorite political candidate without the restrictions of disclosure laws.

The cover of the group's invitation featured a sketch of not a salmon but a squawfish, identifiable by the drawn-in adipose fin and big lips. U.S. Senate candidate Walt Minnick of Idaho said, "This group certainly chose the right mascot. Both the squawfish and this sham organization prey on young steelhead and salmon on their way to the ocean."

Some people also credit the salmon's spiral toward extinction to simple bureaucratic inertia. The BPA and Corps have been managing the Columbia River system since the 1930s, and institutions don't change easily. Involved in the debate for nearly three decades, Ed Chaney called the problem ideological. "If we retreat from the idea that dams are good, some people believe that the whole system might collapse." If the bureaucracies are inclined to resist change, that resistance is assured by the lobbying of the Columbia River Alliance, through which the industries' biologists, engineers, lawyers, and ad men follow every step of every process affecting BPA and the Corps, making it easy to sustain the status quo and painful to do otherwise. Pushing for substantive change has become tantamount to career suicide for people working in government or industry.

Beyond vested interests and inertia, part of the problem is pride. Ex-governor Cecil Andrus said, "It almost became an athletic contest to see who would win."

Knowing about the formidable problems of

fish and dams, a sensible question at this point is: are the salmon and steelhead still worth saving? Here lies a river of back-to-back reservoirs where fish climb up cement and steel ladders, most salmon and steelhead hatching from incubators where they are fed food pellets and shot up with antibiotics, their downstream journey undertaken in a diesel-powered barge or in a tanker truck snorting down I-84. Why even bother?

At best, it seems we will have a fishery amounting to a mere shadow of what once was. But the same is true everyplace. Ten percent of the Northwest's old-growth forest is left, one percent of America's tallgrass prairie survives, one percent of the grizzly bear habitat remains intact, and now even songbird populations are plummeting. Many people believe that the salmon are worth saving simply because they are still there.

The Indians stand to lose the most—their food source, cultural foundation, and spiritual mainstay are all tied up in these fish. Ted Strong said, "The salmon are one of those creatures that can help us teach ourselves about the hierarchy of life and about the underpinnings and purpose of life. To tribal peoples, that underpinning is not dominion over the earth, but servitude to the earth." Bypassing the fish's significant value as food and as an economic staple of indigenous culture, Strong added, "If we understand our origins in relation to these other life-forms, we'll have the opportunity to develop experiences that are spiritual. It's a comforting side of existence, because our primary experience is with capitalism and democracy. We don't always have experiences with spirituality. In their struggle to survive, the salmon make the human seem pitiful and arrogant, because we boast of our abilities and yet whine about our conditions."

So as long as the trade-off is one of power rates going from 60 percent of the national average to 66 percent, of decreasing subsidies to the aluminum industry that employs 0.2 percent of the workforce, of a two-month inconvenience to the barging industry whose entire existence has stood on taxpayers' shoulders since the first barge was built—when simple moderation of these statistics is what's at risk, why not save the fish? Charles Ray of Idaho Rivers Unlimited said, "We shouldn't be asking, 'Are the fish worth it?' The question is, 'Are the dams worth it?'"

SOLVING THE PROBLEM

Without the lower Snake River dams, we would not be talking about a residual fishery but quite likely a fabulous one. Having pushed the compromise position of a two-month lowering of the Snake River reservoirs and failed, Idaho Rivers United in 1996 advocated dam removal, questioning both the adequacy of a partial drawdown and also the wisdom of compromising with forces so disinclined to compromise in return.

Charles Ray said, "The drawdown is an idea that will not give us certainty of restoring the fish. If the groups on the other side don't want to compromise, then we'll go for the biological certainty of getting rid of the dams. The main thing we'll lose is a seaport in the Rocky Mountains, but does the country or the region really need that? If I wanted a seaport, I'd move to Seattle or Portland rather than expect the taxpayers to bring the seaport to me."

For a bit of perspective on this seemingly extreme position of ripping out the lower Snake

River dams, in the 1950s even the Corps couldn't justify these projects economically, and the boosters in Lewiston couldn't get the congressional votes. The Corps, in fact, consistently opposed construction of dams on the lower Snake because they were uneconomic. After the agency caved in to Lewiston's lobbying pressure and decided to push for construction, Congress repeatedly rejected the proposal because of high costs and hazards to the fish. The cement began to flow only after Washington Senator Warren Magnuson slipped an unnoticed $1 million into a 1955 budget rider to begin work on Ice Harbor Dam. After that, the Corps simply asked for money to complete the chain of dams, ultimately costing taxpayers $1,111,409,000—more than a thousand times the initial appropriation. That is how we got to where we are today.

The four dams can theoretically generate 3,483 megawatts of power, a figure often seen in print. But in fact they never produce that much. Annual production averaged a mere 744 megawatts per year in 1991 through 1994, according to Northwest Power Planning Council data—a little over half of what Northwestern energy conservation programs saved in the late 1980s alone. The four dams provide only 4 percent of the region's electric power, according to annual reports of the utilities. The kilowatt-hours (kwh) generated at the dams were worth about $300 million in 1995 if the same amount of energy were bought from the next most available source. That is less than the amount that BPA claims it spends per year trying to compensate for fish damage from Columbia Basin dams. It's less than the irrigation subsidy, less than the WPPSS debt, and probably less than what the restored fishery would be worth. The Army

Corps projected a total cost of $500 million to breach the dams and drain them permanently— half the cost of rebuilding the fish ladders to draw reservoir levels down for two months each year, a solution that won't solve the problem nearly as well.

With the army Corps of Engineers' data in hand, Boise resident Reed Burkholder championed the cause of dam removal, pointing out that $8 million per year would not be needed to dredge the waterway, which is done entirely at taxpayer expense. An ongoing Snake River "compensation" program of $20 million a year to replace wildlife habitat lost to the dams would not be needed. The Corps' barging program of $52 million a year would be history. Many hatchery costs could be forgotten, and much of the BPA's "avoided cost" of spilling water, amounting to $270 million per year, would be saved. Economist Philip Lansing studied dam elimination and predicted a net *benefit* of $158 million per year to the Northwest economy if inefficient barge subsidies were cut and the BPA's salmon recovery costs were reduced.

In 1996, even a Corps-contracted study found that removal of the Snake River dams was the most economic and effective solution to the salmon problem. HARZA Northwest, an engineering firm, reported that eliminating the dams could cost $75 million a year while current salmon costs top $300 million. "I think we'll eventually see one or more dams go out of service in the next twenty years," said Angus Duncan. "But in the meantime, we'll lose a few more salmon runs."

Another possibility remains to bring this view to the forefront, one that Northwest Power

Planning Council director Ed Sheets likened to a "thermonuclear device." The Native Americans could sue the federal government based on their treaty, which guarantees their right to fish. They can't do that if government dams are killing all the salmon. Landmark cases include Judge George Boldt's ruling in 1974 that Indians had the right to half the salmon catch. A later ruling held that Indians had the right to participate in management of the fishery. A "Boldt III" decision could force the federal government into meaningful action to save the salmon. And it would behoove the taxpayers to do this because, if the fish are allowed to go extinct, a monster of a compensation case will surely result. For the much smaller runs of the upper Columbia above Grand Coulee Dam, the Colville Tribe, which didn't even have a treaty, received $53 million plus $15 million per year for the loss of their salmon.

If the tribes really exercised their rights to force corrective action instead of just settling for federal money after the loss, it wouldn't be beyond

Clear water and a lush riparian corridor along the Metolius River are good for fish, but dams downstream block the historic migration of salmon and steelhead to this stream.

several Northwestern politicians to lash back by trying to break the treaty—yet another episode in an embarrassing national history of swindling the people who once possessed all of the continent. But Charles Ray believes that the nationwide outrage against breaking another treaty would be so great that the Indians' opponents would never get away with it.

Seeking solutions, not conflict, the Indians are reluctant to pursue the treaty path. Ted Strong said, "We have been promised protection for the salmon under the Endangered Species Act. We have not seen the benefits of the full spirit and letter of that measure, but we are giving the government the opportunity to follow the law."

However we bring the salmon back—and the tribes identify a number of choices including drawdown and other measures—Ted Strong believes that leadership is the most crucial ingredient. "We need to bring federal, state, and tribal interests together with one plan for the salmon. The cooperation has to be ordered."

According to the law, the National Marine Fisheries Service (NMFS) has the upper hand in river management because of Endangered Species Act requirements. But in 1996, NMFS reaffirmed its commitment to barging, mimicking the Army Corps approach that has led nowhere but down. "NMFS has been co-opted by the same people that co-opt the Corps and BPA," said Charles Ray. The Hatfield agreement of 1995 not only capped salmon costs but also called for a new regional entity to supersede NMFS and the Power Planning Council and make decisions about the salmon. The BPA's Randy Hardy endorsed this approach and said, "A key impediment so far is the lack of a clear institutional structure."

Others who favor local control cheered the 1995 agreement to get federal fisheries agencies off their backs even though NMFS never really *got* on anyone's back very much. The control, in effect, has always been at the local level. Utilities, the aluminum companies, bargers, and agribusinesses have so controlled decisions that efforts to rescue the salmon have been both limited and shortsighted even though expensive. You might read support for local control as simple opposition to control by fisheries agencies.

As a new authority is contemplated, history is worth learning from. In 1979 NMFS considered listing Snake River salmon as endangered, but the Northwestern congressional delegation circumvented the effort by creating the Northwest Power Planning Council. Historian Keith Petersen believes that the Council was created in part to keep the federal officials at bay. The consensus-based, multistate, science-informed, fifteen-year effort of the Planning Council, promoting citizen participation rather than the usual backroom deals, failed to break the grip of the cheap-electric-power addicts on the Columbia. And before that, Congress in 1965 created the Pacific Northwest River Basin Commission as a regional effort, which for fifteen years produced little but a stack of reports. Each of these new agencies labored for a decade and a half before people gave up on them—a half-generation of delay during which the power users maintained the status quo while the fish proceeded toward extinction. Introducing a new entity each fifteen years could represent a sincere effort to find the correct response through trial and error, or it might just be a bone thrown to fish supporters. In the 1995 case, it might be a deliberate dismantling of the National Marine

Fisheries Service's power just in time to prevent it from being effective, which could easily happen if the agency received strengthened support from the Clinton administration.

People nonetheless hope that a new organization or a reformed Power Planning Council will help. Council Chairman Angus Duncan called for a Columbia Basin Watershed Planning Council with broad responsibilities, including restoration of the river's biological health as the region's first priority. Wendy Wilson of Idaho Rivers United said, "If the new group is made up of the fisheries agencies and the tribes, we might be able to take action to save the fish." But hope waned as the 1995 runs returned in far fewer numbers than any before, as the Republican Congress paralyzed NMFS and the U.S. Fish and Wildlife Service in their endangered species work, and as the subsidized industries rolled over the ratepayers and the fish advocates one more time with new ultra-cut-rates from BPA. In 1996, the staff of the Northwest Power Planning Council recommended that the Council be given executive or legislative authority over the Army Corps of Engineers in its operation of the dams—a solution that could break the pattern of organizational defeat that has repeatedly sent salmon supporters back to square one with a new bureaucracy to establish.

While the question of authority was debated in 1996, eight environmental groups and the Yakama Indian Nation kept the heat turned up by again suing NMFS, the Army Corps, and the Bureau of Reclamation for an inadequate salmon recovery plan and for not implementing the plan they had. Winning the earlier lawsuit seemed to have led to little compliance.

A sad commentary on the times came from Cecil Andrus, who in pushing for the drawdown in 1993 had said, "The salmon must not be permitted to move into extinction." Given the politics of 1996, the ex-governor said, "I do not have much hope. The power brokers and the good-old-boy network are alive and healthy."

But how can we quit while salmon still live?

There are good reasons to not quit. A lot of articles have been written about the "miracle" of irrigation and hydropower, but what about the miracle of this fish that fed people for thousands of years, that nourished a whole ecosystem, that now die by the millions at the hydroelectric turbines? While salmon sells for six dollars a pound in some years, we let the fish decline toward extinction in order to grow crops for which the government pays farmers to curtail production. We kill the fish in order to barge subsidized wheat bound for Asia at taxpayer expense. We drive salmon to extinction so that the aluminum industry can buy power at one-sixth the rate of homeowners nationally, then pack up and move abroad when the market suits them.

CHANGING THE POLITICS

A poll by Columbia River utilities found that 84 percent of Northwesterners agreed the salmon will survive only if we take special steps to protect them; 68 percent said they'd be willing to accept a five-dollar-per-month increase in their electric bills, which is more than is likely needed to save the fish. While constituents were saying this, politicians from the region took the canned approach: "If you want salmon, you can buy them in a can."

While residents pay two to four dollars per

An early summer snowfall whitens the grass near the Salmon River's headwaters. If the problems of the downstream dams can be solved, abundant runs of fish will return to this great Columbia tributary.

month just to support the irrigation subsidies, not to mention all the others, Republican Representative Linda Smith of southern Washington said that the cost of protecting salmon could "leave people unable to pay their heating bills." Senator Slade Gorton favored hundreds of millions of dollars of subsidies for his Political Action Committee contributors while arguing that BPA spends too much on salmon. He suggested that "you let species disappear" if the price of saving them is too high. He proposed to gut the Endangered Species Act nationwide and pushed for a bill to completely exempt salmon from the law. Idaho Senator Dirk Kempthorne sponsored an amendment to freeze new endangered species listings and proposed that compliance with the Endangered Species Act be voluntary on private land. In 1995 Representative Helen Chenoweth argued against protection for salmon in her home state of Idaho and showed a staggering amount of ignorance when she asked in an Associated Press

story if a frozen fillet from Alaska isn't enough proof that salmon survive. She seemed to be unaware that the Alaskan fish are another species, that the Alaskan runs are 1,600 miles away, and that they do nothing for the sportsmen, Indians, ecosystem, or economy of Chenoweth's home state—once the greatest salmon jurisdiction in the country. Tacked onto a budget bill needed for the government to meet essentials such as social security payments in 1995, she proposed to bar NMFS from "on-land activities under the Endangered Species Act," whatever that means.

Democratic Congressman Peter DeFazio of Oregon fought for the salmon against all these people, saying, "I believe this Congress is bought and sold."

Typical of the old guard is Larry Craig of Idaho. His state once benefited from nearly half the Columbia's total fish runs, and 45,000 anglers still bought steelhead licenses in 1993. More than one-fourth of the state's 1.2 million people buy general fishing licenses. By some estimates the 1994–1995 steelhead season resulted in $44 million in benefits to the Idaho economy. This is significant but nothing compared to what a restored fishery would yield. Craig's constituents stood to gain tremendously by steelhead recovery, but he favored his shadow government of barge companies in Washington and Oregon that ship grain overseas, of agribusinessmen from Washington State—Conagra alone gave Craig $11,500 between 1989 and 1996—and of the multinational aluminum companies including Kaiser and Reynolds, which contributed $5,500 to his campaign. These figures don't include individuals affiliated with the industries, nor do they include money given to the Republican Party and spent on

Craig's behalf. It's no surprise that Craig opposed the drawdown. The Idaho *Statesman* on August 2, 1994 reported him saying, "We got caught up in the Western romance of returning the salmon from bank to bank jumping the dams. It was nice romance, but it's romance." Craig backed a timber industry bill for state takeover of federal land dedicated to habitat protection. He fought against federal authority to protect the fish and worked to sabotage the effort, then argued, "We have found that federal authority has, in fact, failed."

While the politicians have changed over time, and will continue to do so, the issues, the influence, and the conflicts remain timeless, all of it proving again and again that people who care about the good things in Northwestern life need to be involved in their future.

Lacking effective action by agencies that are politically hamstrung, only one avenue remained for the survival of the steelhead and salmon: the election of different politicians. In Oregon, the salmon were put to a test in a 1996 election when voters rejected Senate candidate and food processor Gordon Smith, who said he would fight salmon-saving actions that might raise power rates, and he vowed to gut the Endangered Species Act.

Voters instead elected Democratic salmon supporter Ron Wyden and when polled said that environmental issues were a major reason for their vote. Smith ran again, moderated his anti-environmental rhetoric, and won when the other Senate seat was available by a thin margin.

With troubling questions about foresight and greed, it's easy to criticize our ancestors for driving the buffalo to the brink of extinction and killing off species such as the passenger pigeon. Ignorance was among their excuses, but it is not one for the decision makers of today.

How will the future judge people such as Larry Craig and Slade Gorton when history holds that they let the symbol of the Northwest go extinct for the sake of surplus crops, subsidized barges, and cut-rate electricity? Those politicians are set to preside over both the extinction of the region's emblem of life and the triumph of corporate dole.

The people of the Northwest say they want the salmon and steelhead to be spared. Now perhaps they'll elect representatives who likewise believe that we can share the earth with these creatures that have nourished the people so well since the beginning of time.

CHAPTER THREE

THE FORESTS

THE ORIGINAL FOREST

The forests of the Columbia region cover the muscled mountains in a green thickness scented with life and the sweet rot of leafy, woody death and rebirth.

If the rivers are the arteries of the watershed, then the forests are the skin, lungs, digestive tract, waste-purging liver, and a whole group of endocrine glands fine-tuning the greater organism. The body of trees and related soil houses and feeds most of the biomass of the basin, controls runoff, cleanses the impurities in water and air, produces fertile humus, grips the crumbling crust of the earth on the slopes where it belongs, and regulates the temperature, making the place livable and fabulous in its complex beauty.

Vast and diverse, the forest estate of the Columbia appears in four regions. First, at the eastern flank of the Basin, woodlands grow thick on the Rocky Mountains, greening the terrain from edges of alpine meadows down across the western slope and then over the foothills to drylands at

LEFT: *Old-growth forests have been cut until little is left, and efforts to safeguard the remaining ten percent ignited a firestorm of controversy. This protected grove survives along the North Fork of the Middle Fork Willamette River in Oregon.*

Spokane, Lewiston, Boise, and Pocatello. Second, to the far north in the Basin, the forests stretch nearly unbroken across southeastern British Columbia, northern Idaho, and northern Washington. Western red cedar, western hemlock, and western white pine thrive in this rainy region interrupted by ponderosa pine in a drier belt east of the Cascades. Third, at the interior and southern reaches of the watershed, a high, arid steppe surrounds isolated mountain ranges including the Blue and adjoining Wallowa of northeastern Oregon. In these ranges, ponderosa pines rise as stately giants of hot, crackling forests, old trees of four-foot diameter with long-needled crowns shading grasslands and dropping big cones that cover the ground like bushels of unpicked apples. Finally, the western Columbia Basin features the Cascades with some of the most magnificent forests on the continent. The dry east slope houses a parkland of ponderosa, the west side a cloud- and fog-shrouded showcase of incense cedar, Douglas-fir that might live 800 years, and true firs, including noble, Pacific silver, and grand. Adjoining the Cascades in a continuous forest mass, the drippy, tangled woodlands of the Coast Range are full of mixed conifer species with oaks and alders filling important niches of the robust ecosystem.

The wooded cloak of the region can be pictured as an enormous inverted ∪ covering the east, north, and west sides of the greater Pacific Northwest from the Rocky Mountain crest to the ocean, with drylands spotted by forests occupying the inside space. In the amount of biomass produced, the temperate forests of the Northwest are by some estimates four times as productive as the celebrated rainforests of the tropics.

When I first traveled to the Cascades in 1967,

the shaggy mane of enormous trees invited me into the woods. I didn't think of it as old growth, a name that refers to unlogged forests of centuries-old trees of mixed ages and species, with an uneven but shading canopy, dead snags, and decaying logs. Being nineteen and hungry to see the world, I didn't really think much at all as I entered the shady grove, but I was enraptured by what I found. The coolness of it seemed to breathe life into me and into everything inside that great green room of the earth. I had grown up in the woods, building tree houses and helping my brother build log cabins, and hunting with a rifle or shotgun for anything that I was allowed by law to kill. But now, more than ever before, I felt I was truly *in* the woods, with columns of solid giants left and right, with a dome of blue green, yellow green, and every other kind of green catching light above me, and a ground cover of interwoven roots, matted needles, and spongy dirt. The smell was organic, the light softly filtered, the sound muffled and calming.

Later that day I hiked up to the tops of the Cascade peaks, and saw that the ragged texture of dark, old trees lay deep and wide. Today, however, a sea of clear-cuts fills the view. With a dusting of snow seen from the air, the logged acreage looks more like a checkerboard than the mazed mosaic of forestland seen relatively intact only a generation ago.

Like the salmon, the forests have been reduced until pathetically little of their original wealth remains. Clear-grained wood once fueled a vigorous economy, but the finest we had was marketed and sold, and now it's gone. Struggling in a landscape as fractured as the Columbia River is by dams, keystone species of wildlife approach the brink of extinction because they find so few old woodlands in which to live.

The logging industry followed the now-obsolete gold mines and salmon canneries to become a principal economic machine of the region until the 1990s, and the fate of logging now reflects the fate of the other two enterprises. In all three cases, resources that people once depended upon have been exhausted. The pace of cutting quickened from the era of crosscut saws and hoofed horsepower to chainsaws, behemoth loaders with six-foot jaws, and helicopters hoisting logs from where they fell and lifting them to idling fleets of growling trucks.

After the private land owned by industrial giants such as Boise Cascade was cut over—the peak harvest on private land occurred in 1952—timber companies in the Northwest turned to land managed by the U.S. Forest Service and owned by all Americans. National forests accommodated the harvest at a rapid-fire rate and an entire society was sustained on the industry of tree falling. Boys would be loggers when they grew up. It came naturally to them. The companies and mills provided steady employment at good wages. The work suited the men. It was hard and physical, with big equipment for big logs. Local businesses provided everything from tear-resistant shirts called Hickories in the uniform of every logger, to $200,000 yarders for dragging the logs by steel cable across the forest floor. The woods had always been there, and cutting and selling it was tantamount to a birthright for small-town Oregonians, Washingtonians, or British Columbians.

People had the idea that this could go on

Logs are stacked for processing in Oregon. While cutting rates soared in the 1980s, big companies eliminated jobs through automation and shipped logs to Japan. Meanwhile the supply of big timber dwindled because it had been cut much faster than it grew.

forever. They expected it. They depended on it, as did the people who had relied on New England textile mills until the 1960s, Pittsburgh steel mills until the 1970s, and the General Motors factory in Flint, Michigan, where 30,000 workers were laid off in one year in the 1980s. Closer to home, Boeing terminated 25,000 Seattle workers in the early 1990s. Unlike those other industries, the demise of logging was heartlessly predictable. Simply put, the big trees were being cut faster than they grew.

For one hundred years, logging had not been much questioned in the Northwest. To do so would be at your own peril. But after a century of cutting, nearly all the originally standing trees were gone, and then it seemed that everything came into question—everything from ecosystems and the international balance of trade to unemployment checks and violence at home.

Had the industry cut every acre of old growth and then run out—completely out—the loss of the jobs and mills would simply have been another in a long line of predictable economic busts and American tragedies that people of the past seemed to regard as inevitable, ranking right up there with the liquidation of Appalachian forests and coalfields, the fished-out Chesapeake Bay, or the exploited soil in Deep South cotton fields. Left alone at the 1980s' rate of harvest, the timber companies would have cut it all by about the year 2000. Then the workers would likely resent, without recourse, the fast pace at which they had been ordered to log. But in the Northwest, a movement to save a remnant of the majestic old forest was born, and it thrived, growing to a social movement of powerful proportions. With 10 percent of the old growth in the

Northwest remaining, forest advocates declared a war to save the environment, and by unfortunate association it became a social and cultural war.

Conservationists convinced Congress to protect some wooded tracts, such as French Pete Valley in the McKenzie basin of Oregon, but according to ecologist Elliott Norse, only 6 percent of the Northwest's original old growth was set aside in wilderness, parks, or other protected areas by 1990, and most of that was in higher, less productive country rather than in rich and temperate lowlands. The cutting continued on the unprotected acreage, and as the percentage of remaining old forest grew smaller, the opposition to sawing it down grew larger. The social discord became more jarring, the political stakes more consequential, and the flow of money to leverage decisions more blatant.

At exactly the time when old-growth forests were undeniably running short and while activists were mobilizing to stop the loss of what little remained, Ronald Reagan became president, and the last big hurrah of Northwestern logging began. John Crowell, vice president and general counsel for the forest products' giant Louisiana Pacific, was appointed Assistant Secretary of Agriculture in charge of the Forest Service. He pushed the agency to even higher cutting rates, saying he believed the nationwide annual harvest could double by 1990.

Knowing better, some Forest Service officials had been trying to reduce cuts, not increase them. In 1983, nine Forest Service supervisors warned Chief Max Peterson that the rate of cutting could not continue. In 1989, forest supervisors from northwestern states wrote to Chief Dale Robertson that the agency was "out of control." Once retired, Northwest Regional Forester James Torrence in an *Oregonian* interview attributed Crowell's goal to "living out there in fantasy land." Living in a land of timber industry campaign contributions, Oregon Senator Mark Hatfield and Representative Les AuCoin also pressed for more logging. While most people thought we had protected public land from the timber barons early in the century when the national forests were created by the likes of Teddy Roosevelt, the Northwestern cut in the early 1980s exceeded growth by 61 percent or more. From 1987 through 1989, a record amount of timber was cut from federal land throughout Oregon and Washington. Congress ordered cuts of up to 1 billion board feet per year in excess of what the Forest Service had recommended (a board foot is one foot square and one inch thick; an average home can be built with 10,000 board feet). In 1990, pleading for some self-restraint and foresight, Forest Service Chief Dale Robertson, in an understatement, told a House Agriculture Subcommittee, "We know that the unusually high harvest levels of the past three years in the Pacific Northwest cannot continue."

Funds for harvest and logging roads were increased well beyond the amounts the Forest Service requested and funds for ecological research were withheld by members of Congress who trimmed to the bone the budgets for knowledge but cut not a penny for logging or industrial subsidies. New information was not welcome if it didn't support increased logging. One project that had started in 1982 to provide forest managers with data they needed to comply with requirements of the 1976 National Forest Management Act was reduced from $10 million to $2 million,

saving a sum that pales in relation to subsidies for even single logging companies. A carefully structured planning process, arising out of lawsuits against clear-cutting and gruesome public land management of the 1960s and 1970s, lay in the doldrums of deliberate administrative delay while public timber was liquidated at any cost. A sawdust blizzard set unrealistic expectations for the future, including an inflated harvest figure against which any sustainable cut would look disappointing and inadequate. Enjoying this binge of prosperity while it lasted, the workers of the Northwest were betrayed by the politicians who accelerated the cut for corporate constituents wanting short-term profits more than anything else.

In every way, the machine of established power connived to get out the cut. Inventory data was both innocently and clandestinely falsified, duping people into believing there were more old-growth trees than in fact existed. The most devious of these phantom forest calculations lay in the northern Rockies where agency officials went so far as to keep two computer inventories of the forest—one for use and one for show. An exposé by Liz Sedler in *Wild Forest Review* indicated that in the Kootenai National Forest, only 61 percent of the "mature timber" was really there. West of the Cascades, the Forest Service reported in the late 1980s that 4.1 million acres of old growth remained, but Peter Morrison, a forest ecologist commissioned by The Wilderness Society, conducted comprehensive studies by using federal agency data and sophisticated geographic information-systems mapping. He concluded that only 2.3 million acres of old growth survived, down from an original 20 million acres in western Oregon and

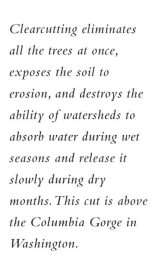

Clearcutting eliminates all the trees at once, exposes the soil to erosion, and destroys the ability of watersheds to absorb water during wet seasons and release it slowly during dry months. This cut is above the Columbia Gorge in Washington.

people failed through a kind of civic paralysis to stem the tide of loss—so too were the 1980s the decade of disaster for Northwestern forests. Activists who were determined to stop logging of the most valuable sites threw themselves into the battle and confronted belligerent opposition and a political monolith of calculated resistance to change.

A NEW AWARENESS

Logging had been happening since the first days of white settlement, but the modern extent of cutting and poor harvest practices had led to scarcity, and with it a broadened awareness of the forest as a barometer and governor of environmental health. For example, the rivers and streams depend on wise management of the forests, and they reflect what is done throughout their watersheds. In this regard, the Northwestern floods of 1996 made a fitting capstone to the era of wholesale clear-cutting in the Pacific Northwest. The highest water since 1964 resulted from a lot of rain, but the severity of flooding was far worse than it might have been. After logging, snow accumulates deeper in clear-cuts than it does in a forest and is more likely to melt all at once, especially with rainstorms. The once seamless forest floor of organic humus, rotting logs, and sponge-like mattresses of needles had been scraped, compacted, bulldozed, and burned, and on many mountainsides replaced with bare dirt. Sheltering the soil, a canopy of needled crowns two hundred feet high once rose above the tops of small- and medium-sized trees of diverse types, but it was gone. The root masses probing deep into the soil and creating minute conduits for water to pene-

Washington. The difference was significant considering that 71,000 acres per year were being logged in the 1980s from national forests of the two states. Logging had fragmented much of the remaining unprotected old growth into islands of eighty acres or smaller, providing sparse habitat for the species that needed it. Less than 20 percent of the remaining old growth lay in low-elevation forests that supported the most productive and diverse ecosystems. The amount has decreased further in recent years. The rate of logging had skyrocketed, far beyond any remotely sustainable level that could have given workers and forest communities a stable future.

Just as history shows the 1980s being the lost decade for the salmon—ten years during which

trate into the earth were also gone. All of those losses caused runoff to peak much higher.

Logging roads winding like the scribbles of a child now slashed the mountainsides. The roads bled natural reservoirs of groundwater from underneath and sluiced the runoff by ditch to the nearest streams, which instantly became over-loaded with flushed-off rainwater, snowmelt, and groundwater. The streams swelled to the bursting point, chewed violently on their banks, and raged with logs as battering rams through the valleys to larger streams, until the normally gentle Willa-mette carried a shocking volume equivalent to the Columbia's average flow.

University of Washington hydrologist Dennis Harr found that clear-cuts he surveyed produced ten times the runoff of uncut forests. Even estab-lished young forests produced 40 percent more runoff than old forests. A Forest Service study by Gordon Grant and Julia Jones showed peak runoff from surveyed clear-cut areas increasing by half. The roads are often the biggest culprit, and a study by Northwest Environmental Watch in Seattle, using agency data, found that the logging road network totaled more than 73,000 miles in Oregon, 22,000 in Washington, 33,000 in Montana, and 150,000 in British Columbia. Northwestern national forests contain 3.5 miles of road for every square mile of land—the equivalent of a road every 500 yards in parallel lines across the landscape—the frequency of major cross streets in a city and twice the density known to cause population declines in elk, grizzly bears, and wolves. The roads and adjacent bulldozing in a typical logging area consume 8 percent of the land and eliminate all associated trees. The road system alone on commercial forestland in

Washington, Oregon, and northern California consumes 2.4 million acres—two times the size of Delaware. Erosion of soil has always happened, but erosion in roaded areas can occur at one hundred times the natural rate, according to sources researched by Environmental Watch.

A clear illustration of the problem lay in northern Idaho, where the January rainstorms of 1996 caused 295 landslides, many of them in logged areas sliced by haul roads. One slide in the North Fork Clearwater basin dumped 500,000 tons of earth into Quartz Creek and ruined it. Depending on taxpayers to fix the damage, the Forest Service asked the Federal Highway Administration for $8 million to repair the roads, but the streams couldn't *be* repaired. Only time, without additional stresses of logging, will do that. One month later, in a decision that outraged fisheries groups, the Forest Service proposed to log 27 more million board feet of timber from the same degraded area.

Damage to the land affects not only the quantity of runoff but quality of water as well. Slow seepage of rainwater and snowmelt through the duff of decomposing plants, fallen needles, and rotting trees is a perfect, free filtration system that yields clean water. But the runoff of scoured clear-cuts and road cuts rips at the soil and erodes it with muddy flows, which silts over gravel beds needed by invertebrate life and spawning fish. Siltation from poorly managed logging is one of the main reasons for the decline of salmon and steelhead, as well as the disappearing bull trout, the imperiled Dolly Varden trout, and others. Ed Sheets of the Northwest Power Planning Council said, "Even if we do fix the dams on the Columbia and Snake Rivers, we will have to repair spawning habitat in streams if we are to succeed in restoring the salmon and steelhead."

Silt generated by logging reduces the amount of light available to beneficial underwater plants, and contaminates city water supplies. After one-fourth of Bull Run basin in Hood River National Forest was logged, Portland's water supply failed to meet health standards during the 1996 flood. A sediment filtration plant could cost $200 million, funded not by the logging companies that caused the damage but by everyone who turns the tap in the Columbia Basin's largest city.

With one of the more comprehensive views toward stream protection, in 1994 the Pacific Rivers Council called for adoption of a watershed strategy to apply new conservation standards on all federal land and to educate the public about the need for better forest management. The Council stressed protection of the best remaining habitat, followed by restoration of streams adjoining the unspoiled areas and ultimately linking recoverable habitat between refuges. A reunited ecosystem is the final goal. "We need to first protect the best areas and then reestablish the connection between our streams and their floodplains," said Council spokesman Bob Doppelt.

Restoration includes reinstating large woody debris in the streams to replace giant logs that used to fall across the water and create pools, riffles, and an important nutrient base for stream life. "If we didn't have wood in our streams, we wouldn't have fish to speak of," said ecologist Chris Maser. Riverbank shade, lowland overflow areas, and wildlife corridors are all important

At the Yakima River's headwaters near Snoqualmie Pass, whole blocks of forest, despite their location on steep slopes, have been clearcut on industry-owned land. Little habitat remains for wildlife that is dependent on old-growth conditions.

features in the forest and water interface.

The relationship to floodplains and water is only one illustration of a forest linkage that is critical to life on earth. From the highest breezy treetop to the deepest root underground, the forest is a web of life on which many creatures and the health of the whole landscape depend. Even when it's not raining, needles at the tops of trees collect moisture from the damp Northwestern air and allow it to drip down and be used by plants, accounting for 35 percent of the forest's moisture in one study at Bull Run. Lichens growing in high treetops blow down in the winter to make essential feed for deer when other food sources are buried by snow. The forest canopy creates warm areas in winter and cool areas in summer; the forest is a refuge for wildlife during times of climatic stress.

Even more than the airy canopy of the forest, the ground underfoot is a hotbed of life. One square meter of forest soil can contain 2,000 earthworms, 40,000 insects, 120,000 mites, 120 million nematodes, and very large numbers of protozoa and bacteria. Far from being a sterile dirt pile whose purpose is merely to be stood upon or hold up trees as if they were big toothpicks stuck in clay, the soil is an alive mass of organisms vital to forest health. Mycorrhizae fungi cling to root hairs of the trees, where they are needed to provide phosphorus, nitrogen, and antibiotics against parasites. An estimated 95 percent of the fungi disappear when a forest is clear-cut. By disturbing and destroying soil, poorly managed logging sows the seeds of its own destruction. We can talk about forests being renewable, but as conservationist Timothy Coleman questioned, "What will the next forest grow *on*?"

Ecologist Jerry Franklin of the University of Washington calls for a new forestry that recognizes the connections between soil, trees, and the rest of the ecosystem and allows them to function while still cutting selectively. Franklin's forestry leaves woody debris on the ground to rot and contribute to the nutrient cycle. It spares snags and allows big rotting logs to stay in place. It minimizes road building. It costs more than clear-cutting because more care is taken, and it yields fewer logs in the short run because the forest is not liquidated all at once. But it offers the significant promise of having both forests and logs for tomorrow. Efforts to protect remaining old growth dominated forest-related controversies in the 1990s because of scarcity and imminent threat, but in the future, management strategies such as new forestry will likely be the focus of forest reform as people sort out ways to use the woods sustainably and to restore lost qualities.

Emblematic of ancient Northwestern forests, the spotted owl feeds on flying squirrels and western red-backed voles that thrive in decaying logs—and a fallen Douglas-fir, if left alone, will decay for five hundred years. The vole's diet, in turn, is comprised of truffles, the underground fruiting bodies of the fungi that live in beneficial association with tree roots. Vole droppings include fungi spores and thus spread the truffles. The trees provide for the truffles, which feed the voles, which feed the owls, which nest in the dead trees and keep the voles in check. All of these members of a healthy forest depend on each other, and this is only one among many circles of life in the woods.

Each pair of owls was thought to need 1,200 to 3,000 acres of old growth, and their threatened status in 1990 created the greatest endangered

Moose and other species need a healthy riparian corridor for much of their food supply and shelter. Setback requirements have rarely been adequate to protect the forests along rivers and streams.

species debate of all time. It has exceeded the intensity of the salmon debate because activities causing the salmon's extinction have been changed only in token ways, thus muting the controversy while allowing extinction to proceed.

Once forest advocates gained public attention through the Endangered Species Act, they strove to point out that the owl was only a symptom of a far greater problem: an entire ecosystem had been affected to the degree that it can no longer support native Northwestern life. About 667 species of plants and animals are found in old growth of the Northwest, and 482 of those are closely associated with it, according to Forest Service studies. And the values of the old-growth ecosystem don't simply grow back the way cellulose grows on trees. As described by Elliot Norse in *Ancient Forests of the Pacific Northwest,* it takes hundreds of years to produce the mix of micro- and macro-organisms that characterize old growth, and the mix will never be reconstituted if the species dependent on the remaining shreds of uncut forests are allowed to go extinct. Both this body of life and the ultimate productivity of the soil for sawlogs are doomed if changes in forest management don't occur. It's not only the owl that's threatened. It's the life of the Northwest—the essence of it—the health of the entire forest ecosystem.

THE PAINFUL STAGE OF TRANSITION

The threat is not logging per se, but rather the systematic logging of every last bit of old growth that remains. The forests are cut because the timber industry makes money, but anyone who seriously considered the rate of cutting in the 1980s knew about the Achilles heel of sustainability. In long-term context, the 10 percent of old growth remaining in the Northwest is nothing but a blip on the chart of logging history, and the remaining sawlogs are relatively insignificant to the total forest economy. If the old trees were all cut, we would then be in the same quandary that we are in now—only ten years later, when everyone would have to face the same problem of economic transition but without any ancient forest left for genetic reserves, ecosystem stability, watershed protection, human heritage, or recreation. Second-growth timber—not the residual old growth—is now the basis of a continued logging economy, and that would be true with or without cutting the old growth that remains.

While the rate of cutting increased phenomenally in the 1980s and sent log trucks wheeling down the mountain roads in what seemed like bumper-to-bumper traffic for a few years, timber industry employment did not increase. It decreased. Automation in the mills on the west side of the Cascades forced the layoff of 30,000 workers during a ten-year period. In America's greatest forest belt—the Pacific slope in Oregon, Washington, and northern California—timber-related jobs totaled 10 percent of all employment in 1970 but declined to 5 percent during the timber-cutting frenzy of the 1980s, and the percentage continued to fall. While timber-related employment declined and mill towns suffered, profits of the large logging companies skyrocketed; Weyerhaeuser reached a profit record of $372 million in 1992. While the output of finished timber increased by 19 percent in the 1980s, employment dropped 14 percent. Loss of another 30,000 jobs is expected over the next twenty years owing to efficiency increases at the mill. In the industry's defense, the labor-saving automation made the business more competitive in an international marketplace; the companies argue that some jobs were sacrificed to save others.

With no such justification, thousands more workers were laid off because timber companies exported unmilled logs to Japan. In the late 1980s, about 40 percent of all timber cut in Washington went overseas, and in the early 1990s nearly a quarter of the timber from the Northwest was exported. For raw logs, the Japanese paid two or three times the price bid by American mills. In 1990, when 3.6 million board feet of raw logs were exported from the Northwest, a Forest Service report found that milling the logs generated three times the number of jobs of exporting them. The agency recommended a ban on log exports to create 15,000 jobs. But it didn't happen.

While the exports flowed in 1989 and 1990, forty-eight mills closed in Oregon, Washington, and Idaho, causing 5,500 workers to lose their jobs. Foreseeing an impending scarcity owing to the fact that the old growth of clear and tightly grained wood has been cut so fast, the Japanese sink whole logs in harbors to preserve them for future use and soaring value—something we could have achieved simply by not cutting as fast as we did. The Japanese will later process and sell our trees back to us at inflated prices.

Although log export is banned for trees cut on U.S. government land—with the enormous exception of Alaska—logs from private and state land go straight to freighters bound overseas in a pattern often associated with resource colonies in the Third World. But in fact, it's worse than that. The United States is the only country in the Pacific Rim to allow export of unprocessed logs. Even the Philippines protects its timber workers by requiring that logs be processed at home. America once again serves as a resource colony, not controlled by King George of England this time, but by Japan, in a relationship secured by political influence of the timber industry. Correcting this situation has immense popular appeal; Oregon residents voted nine to one to ban log exports from state land in 1989. Representative Peter DeFazio of Oregon sponsored legislation to reduce exports of raw logs and to eliminate $100 million per year in subsidies going to the export market, but his bill failed to overcome industry-backed opposition. In spite of their rhetoric, politicians other than a few such as DeFazio represented timber owners and not workers.

Aggravating an already bad situation, many of the small mills in the 1960s through 1980s were crowded out by big mills, which were able to outbid the family operations on which the all-American mystique of Northwestern logging stood. Plum Creek Timber—a giant in the industry though its name sounds quaint—cut ravenously from its 1.5 million acres of private holdings inherited from the free federal giveaway of forests to the Northern Pacific Railroad during Abe Lincoln's presidency. For every mile of track built, the federal government gave the railroad 25,600 acres, free. Cutting this acreage in the 1980s and exporting the logs to Japan at windfall profits, the company stripped its property bare in 640-acre clear-cuts and then in the 1990s turned to the national forests of Idaho and Montana. With its Japanese proceeds in hand, the company outbid local Montana sawmills in Polson, Kalispell, and Whitefish until they folded, leaving Plum Creek with the corner on the market.

While the sawlog-quality forests dwindled, and machinery replaced jobs, and timber owners shipped their logs straight to Japan for milling, and multinational corporations squeezed small sawmills out of business, the loggers' woes were exasperated by growing public sentiment to stop cutting the small amount of old growth that remained. Forest activists filed appeals on virtually every major sale and delayed many, which was all the industry needed to cultivate an image of scapegoat. In the politics of lumber, it was not automation, or exports, or an exhausted supply of trees that would take the public relations hit. Industry officials blamed their ills on the forest activists and, following that lead, the loggers found in the "tree huggers" an easier target than the lucrative but antilabor policies of their employers.

On this painful stage of transition, becoming increasingly cultural in context, protests and direct action from Earth First! and other groups heightened the old-growth debate. People climbed trees and sat in them for days to prevent cutting, chained themselves to road gates, and lay in front of log trucks. Some activists vandalized logging equipment and spiked trees to discourage sawing. The loggers couldn't fight the exports but they could fight a bunch of defenseless "hippies" in the woods. Protesters were intimidated, beaten up, shot at, fined, and jailed, yet they continued to protest.

While forest activists occupied the barricades and the spotted owl was being considered for endangered status in 1987, the Forest Service sold a record 5.6 billion board-feet in Oregon and Washington. Then the rate of cutting began to decline as the long-awaited forest plans finally went into effect after years of delay by the Reagan administration. In the wake of the plans, one scientific study after another confirmed the scarcity and importance of old-growth habitat and ratcheted the recommended cut downward. With other options squandered, crisis management was the only brand of management left, and Congressional members, including Jim Jontz of Indiana, drew up legislation to protect remaining ancient forest stands. But the bills, designed to avert a full-blown endangered species confrontation, were stonewalled by the Northwest delegation, which was willing to gamble everything in order to keep cutting at a rapid rate for a few more years.

Pressed by the Endangered Species Act, the Forest Service finally conducted a biological study for a definitive estimate of how much old growth needed to be set aside or managed compatibly for the spotted owl. In 1990 the prestigious Jack Ward Thomas committee reported that 7.1 million acres were necessary; 3.1 million of it were already slated for commercial harvest. The next year, the Fish and Wildlife Service was forced by the courts to comply with the Endangered Species Act and reported that 11.6 million acres of old growth were needed. Still the logging continued. Court action was required to get the agencies to obey the law.

In 1991, forest advocacy groups won a decisive lawsuit when Judge William Dwyer virtually shut down new logging in spotted owl habitat until federal agencies complied with the Endangered Species Act. Recognizing that agency scientists had for seventeen years warned the Forest Service of legal conflict because of the condition of the owls' habitat, the judge ruled that the agencies had engaged in a "deliberate and systematic refusal to comply with the laws protecting wildlife." The judge recognized that the problem was not with Forest Service officials trying to do their jobs, but rather reflected decisions made by higher authorities in the executive branch of government. Forest advocates finally had a firm legal grip to slow the tide of loss.

President George Bush's response to this complex set of economic, ecological, legal, and cultural problems was to declare jobs more important than owls. "We'll be up to our necks in owls and every millworker will be out of a job," he said while campaigning in 1992. Pushing a moderate view, Bill Clinton won in Oregon, Washington, and California. By no means a dead industry, logging companies cut 9.6 billion board feet from all lands in Oregon and Washington in 1993, down from a ten-year average of 13.2 billion board feet but not a radical reduction considering how excessive the cut had been.

THE NORTHWEST FOREST PLAN

On taking office, President Clinton called for a face-to-face timber summit with representatives of all factions in the struggle over old growth of the western Cascades and Coast Range. A commitment to compromise led to the Northwest Forest Plan.

This protected some remaining ancient forests but let many trees be logged in the 24 million acres of federal forest land of the northern spotted owl region. Supporters said that the plan would protect more forest acreage than any forest planning program had ever done anywhere. It estab-

lished a network of 164 key watersheds in the Northwest and a strategy that incorporated riparian reserves along 2.2 million acres of waterfront, 29 percent of which was old growth. Total reserves of 7.1 million acres were established, but less than half the acreage was covered with old trees, and some thinning and salvage sales would be allowed even in the reserves. The plan identified 3.2 million acres for "experimental" or "innovative" forestry, and offered 4.9 million acres for less limited cutting. Even under this compromise, federal officials recognized that the chances of saving the owl were an uncertain 80 percent.

Andy Kerr of the Oregon Natural Resources Council and others argued for a plan that would protect more trees. "With so little old growth left," Kerr stated, "the compromises have already been made." Bolstering their view, a 1994 report by biologists from the University of Oregon, University of Washington, and Colorado State University cast "serious doubt" that the owl could survive "any additional habitat loss."

Both sides in the contentious forest fight grappled with the president's compromise and sued the government over the Plan. The Oregon Natural Resources Council and others maintained that logging would proceed on a third of the remaining old-growth acres outside parks and wilderness areas and would allow new roads in key watersheds. Meanwhile, their lawsuit continued to prevent any logging in spotted owl forests. To get the environmental groups to drop the suit so that the Northwest Forest Plan could be implemented, the White House threatened to go to the Democratic Congress of 1994 to override environmental restrictions. The courts later upheld the President's Plan. With adoption of it in 1994, the three-year injunction against cutting in spotted owl habitat on public land was lifted. The new plan allowed for 1 billion board feet of old-growth logging—a 75 percent reduction from the inflated 1980s harvest levels—but still a lot given the scarcity of old growth. The plan did not restrict logging on private land, which once constituted 58 percent of the owl's range. Other cases under the Endangered Species Act would address this issue, though virtually all old growth on private land had already been cut.

The protests stopped, the mills adjusted, and a truce seemed to be in effect. For a while, there was hope that the war of the woods had ended. Forest advocates had relaxed since the Dwyer injunction and did not effectively extend their campaign of direct action, agency lobbying, and courtroom finesse into electoral politics. But while they were gaining ground toward forest protection, the politics of forests got worse. In the fall of 1994, Republicans took control of both the U.S. House and Senate, and their platform in the West was straightforward: increase logging. As with the case of the salmon, no amount of legal triumph could defend the forests against a political monolith taking its orders directly from the resource industries.

By summer 1995, nearly 870 million board feet in the spotted owl region of western Oregon and Washington had been legitimately cut under the President's Plan. Another billion board feet were ready to harvest, according to Forest Service reports. But that was not enough to suit the timber industry, and so lobbyists were crawling all over Capitol Hill. The days of the logging truce were numbered.

Even though the cutting of old growth had been stopped for three years and then resumed at a slower pace, the dreaded economic apocalypse never occurred. To the contrary, the economy of the Northwest boomed as never before. Federal planners had expected a loss of 9,000 jobs, but only 4,500 timber jobs were lost (industry representatives had said that 100,000 jobs could be lost). According to Forest Service analyst Kent Connaughten, more significant losses never materialized because private forests filled the gap and secondary manufacturing of wood products grew. Unrelated to logging, people in great numbers immigrated from other states, construction increased to provide for the waves of new residents, the electronics business expanded beyond any boosters' dreams, and a wave of tourism and recreation fueled a regional economic engine that dwarfed the plight of laid-off timber workers. In 1995, tourism alone brought $4 billion to Oregon's economy, approaching the $5.5 billion from the timber industry. Though loggers in many areas did lose their jobs, overall unemployment in the Northwest hit its lowest level in two decades, and many new jobs were available. Even with timber industry layoffs, the two states gained 932,000 jobs in ten years. Even before the injunction against old-growth cutting in the 1990s, timber-related jobs had dropped to less than 3 percent of Washington's employment and only slightly more in Oregon. The sawmill-dominated Santiam Valley of Oregon saw its industry decline, but its school enrollments and property values increased for the first time in many years. All studies indicated that the Northwest's impressive economic boom was linked to quality-of-life issues hinging on the region's remaining forests, rivers, and natural landscape.

THE EASTSIDE ECOSYSTEM

With the uneasy truce in the west side forests of the Cascades, attention of conservationists, government agencies, and the logging industry turned to the more expansive land of the eastern Cascades, Blue Mountains of eastern Oregon, Okanogan Highlands of eastern Washington, and northern Rockies of Idaho and Montana.

The Blue Mountains once supported a five-million-acre parkland of regal ponderosa pine shading velvety grasslands in dry, open glades. The mammoth, old trees provided reservoirs of genetic quality with den sites for animals and nest sites for birds. The issues here differed from the wet western Cascades. The trees took longer to grow: a Douglas-fir required 230 years to reach the size of a 60-year-old on the west side. Regeneration was more difficult in this inter-mountain belt of drier country between the Cascades and Rockies, and so the elimination of old growth was in some ways even more consequential than on the west side.

Only 10 to 15 percent of the old growth remained, and less than a fourth of that amount was protected. An alarming 80 percent of the remaining old-growth patches covered less than one hundred acres according to a compendium of data generated by scientists and published by The Wildlife Society. Systematic high-grading, or culling out the largest trees, had been rationalized by foresters' century-old dogma that in clearing all the old growth, a younger, more vigorous forest would provide a faster-growing supply of lumber. But the opposite occurred. A healthy forest failed to grow back in this dry country. Unsustainable levels of cutting also resulted from an overestimation of old-growth volume and promotion of large sales to entice private investment. Historian Nancy Langston pointed out that even in the 1920s, Forest Service planners knew what politicians in the 1980s refused to recognize: that harvest levels would collapse by the 1990s. Sure enough, the cut from the three Blue Mountain national forests plummeted from 706 million board feet per year in the late 1980s to less than 100 million in 1993. And the forests that remained were markedly degraded.

Key to the health of the forest and entire ecosystem, small lightning-caused fires had historically burned every eight to fifteen years through the big pines, scarcely scarring them but cleaning out brush and favoring healthy grasslands beneath the trees. However, fire suppression and logging had led to undergrowth tinder and dog hair stands of two thousand spindly fir trees per acre, all of it a fuel box for catastrophic fires that incinerate even the organic reservoir of the soil. Although fir trees had gained advantage in germination after the girthy pines were hauled off to mills, they were less suited to the dry environment and hopelessly prone to insect damage compared to the thick-barked pines.

In the new scrubby forest, infestations of tussock moth and pine beetles ran rampant. In the past, the big trees had resisted insect damage because their roots could reach deep groundwater during droughts and thereby continue to produce insect-deterring resin. Small fires and natural succession had earlier created a mosaic of species and ages less susceptible to insects because of a variety in trees. Each different species or age class of trees formed, in effect, a barrier to the infestations of insects, which favor monocultures. Mixed forests had accommodated songbirds that ate the insects,

and large dead trees housed woodpeckers and other insect predators. But that entire system was disrupted, and the resulting forest struggled against problems for which it was unequipped.

The Blue Mountains illustrated what Jack Ward Thomas called the "collapse of an ecosystem" when he undertook research there before conducting his spotted owl studies and stepping up as chief of the Forest Service in 1993. Ecologists agreed that forests in the intermountain region and Rockies needed frequent small burns, but convincing the general public of the benefits proved difficult after a century of heroic fire fighting.

In tandem with the lack of fire, logging and uncontrolled grazing had almost everywhere inflicted stream damage on the interior region. Waterways in federal cutover land suffered from siltation and a 30 to 70 percent reduction of deep pools, essential for fish and other life. Although 75 percent of all Western terrestrial wildlife species need the riparian zones, logging and grazing had degraded 80 percent of riparian areas overseen by the Bureau of Land Management. Elevated water temperatures suffocated fish and bottom life. Banks eroded under the hooves of cows, and ranchers diverted flows for pasture. Some rivers, such as the Powder in eastern Oregon, were completely dried up. In eastern Washington and Oregon, 40 percent of the fifty-two fish species were at risk.

Terrestrial species were in trouble as well. Three-toed woodpeckers required mature lodgepole pines, the fur-bearing fisher needed large, undisturbed acreage and fallen trees with cavities for dens, and the marten favored decaying logs and rotting stumps for shelter. One study in northeastern Oregon found that 178 vertebrate species used fallen logs as habitat.

Arising from the Northwest Forest Plan and pressure by conservation groups that appealed dozens of timber sales, federal agencies in 1994 adopted PACFISH, a set of land use rules for salmon and steelhead streams running through public land on the Pacific slope of the Cascades. The program aimed to limit damage from logging, grazing, mining, and recreation along thousands of miles of streams and avoid the need for more listings under the Endangered Species Act. A similar INFISH program expanded the concept of stream corridor protection to the Inland West, and the Forest Service adopted a system of environmental screens for analyzing new timber sales.

None of the efforts, however, dealt with forest and management practices along low-elevation, private-land rivers, which is where the finest original habitat was. To cope with this political bombshell, the Rivers Council of Washington set a goal of establishing watershed councils in all sixty-two major watersheds of that state. Councils are made up of a full cross section of the community, with members who are determined to work together. Encouraged by a state-sponsored Watershed Health program, forty councils were started in western Oregon. Similar action on the state's rural east side was difficult, yet twenty councils had become active there by 1996.

Documenting a host of problems east of the Cascades, a panel of biologists studied the forests of eastern Oregon and Washington and in a report published by The Wildlife Society recommended protection of roadless areas and old growth, improved management of riparian areas, and restoration of streams and watersheds. With many

of the same findings, a 1995 report commissioned by Governor John Kitzhaber of Oregon recommended protection of old ponderosa pines and riparian areas, and the cutting of smaller, crowded trees by timber companies. Foresters hoped to replicate some of the effects of natural fire by culling out thick stands, leaving large trees, and burning the ground cover under controlled conditions to simulate what nature used to do for free.

To deal more thoroughly with the gamut of forest and public-land problems in the Columbia Basin east of the Cascades, President Clinton had directed that the agencies prepare a "scientifically sound and ecosystem-based strategy for management of east-side forests." The Forest Service and Bureau of Land Management began the Interior Columbia Basin Ecosystem Management Project. This massive undertaking sought to avoid future endangered species conflicts and improve public land stewardship in Oregon, Washington, Idaho, and Montana.

Science costs money, and after $30 million was spent on a draft Interior Columbia document recommending better management of riparian areas and other reforms, Representative George Nethercutt and Senator Slade Gorton of Washington and others in the 1995 Congress tried to eliminate the study's budget before the federal team produced a document with teeth and binding recommendations on the federal agencies. Legislators engaged in this effort made no bones about their desire to also gut the Endangered Species Act, the Clean Water Act, and other protections, the need for which was becoming increasingly evident with each scientific study.

Environmental groups had placed hope in the

LEFT: *Fire, such as this blaze at Yellowstone, has a crucial role in maintaining forest ecosystems. Suppression of natural fires has led to monocultures prone to insect outbreaks, invasion of noxious plants, and accumulation of brush that eventually ignites and causes extremely hot fires.*

Interior Columbia Project, but in October 1995 they responded to the attempted budget cuts by suing to stop all Forest Service logging in old-growth forests of eastern Oregon and Washington, setting the stage for intensified conflict. The Republican cuts were vetoed by President Clinton in a 1996 appropriations bill, and money was released to complete the Interior Columbia Project.

THE NORTHERN ROCKIES

Large tracts of forest in Idaho, Montana, and Wyoming survive along the backbone of the Rockies. Ponderosa pine shade the dry, lower western slopes. Forests of higher elevations thrive in a colder, wetter climate with up to nine months of snow cover. Lodgepole pine bristle the landscape as far as the eye can see, interspersed with mixed forests of Douglas-fir and Englemann spruce. Whitebark pine and subalpine fir occupy picturesque slopes near timberline, where dwarf forests called krummholz border alpine meadows dazzling with wildflowers. Aspens brighten sunny mountainsides, and cottonwoods and willows line the streams.

While nearly every other region of the country has been logged or developed until only scraps of original nature remain, significant pieces of the northern Rockies survive unchanged. Several blocks of large uncut forest remain and hold international significance: central Idaho, including the Greater Salmon/Selway ecosystem, which is about the size of Ohio; Greater Yellowstone with the upper Snake basin; and Glacier National Park with its contiguous Great Bear Wilderness and Bob Marshall Wilderness. The largest mass of

relatively undisturbed temperate forest in the world lies in the Salmon and Selway roadless areas. Bordering the Salmon River basin, one of the most magnificent uncut forest tracts is called Cove/Mallard, where logging companies have begun 200 planned clear-cuts in 90,000 acres of roadless area after years of standoff by forest advocacy groups.

Idaho holds more wilderness than any other state but Alaska, yet here and in Montana efforts to gain permanent safeguards for 15 million acres of roadless wilderness have failed year after year. Seeking protection for larger swaths of undeveloped land than anybody ever sought before, the Alliance for the Wild Rockies in Missoula, Montana, succeeded in nationalizing these largest intact forest ecosystems by appealing to people across the country. Back at home, polls showed 60 percent of Montanans supported keeping all remaining roadless areas the way they are, yet the so-called wilderness bills that were introduced were in fact *anti*wilderness bills that sought to log land that is temporarily safeguarded.

Reduced timber harvests in the western Cascades had set the stage for increased logging in the northern Rockies. After taking an unprecedented public stand in 1989 against high levels of cutting, the national forest supervisors of the region were systematically replaced, including the much-publicized forced retirements of John Mumma and Ernie Nunn. The Forest Service approved plans calling for 150 new timber sales in Idaho over a period of five years. Montana politicians crafted a wilderness bill to release more than 70 percent of roadless forests to logging, but facing opposition by conservationists, the bill failed.

Like the forests of the Pacific slope and

intermountain region, the forests of the northern Rockies house important endangered communities of life. The woodland caribou of northern Idaho and northeastern Washington ranks as the most endangered large mammal in the United States and depends on large uncut tracts. The grizzly bear's final territory south of Canada can be found here. Waters of the northern Rockies support the last stronghold of the bull trout, which is surviving in only 10 percent of its former range. Reaching twenty pounds and migrating as much as 150 miles up and down the rivers, this indicator species of stream health is endangered in all but official designation. In spite of a built-in constituency of anglers, political pressure from the congressional delegations and the governors of Idaho and Montana prevented its listing out of fear of regulations. The Fish and Wildlife Service proffered the curious excuse that even though the fish was in fact endangered, some eighty other regional species were also on their way to extinction. But those were not listed either, because of a ban by the 1995 Congress on recognition of additional endangered species regardless of how imminent their demise. Regional congressional members eventually failed to extend the ban, which was lifted in 1996. A federal judge ordered the Fish and Wildlife Service to reconsider its refusal to list the bull trout as threatened or endangered.

Dependent on the forests surrounding them, Idaho streams have been the principal spawning grounds for salmon and steelhead. But data analyzed by the Pacific Rivers Council indicated that up to 90 percent of the historic numbers of salmon fry have been eliminated by habitat loss, a problem that matches the dams in severity,

according to the Council. Salmon survival in Idaho is ten to fifty-five times higher in streams without logging, grazing, and mining.

Ironically, almost all timber sales in the Rockies lose money for the government. Except for the cutting of fat sawlogs west of the Cascades, sales from federal land in the Columbia Basin were consistently below cost, meaning the government spent more to build roads, sell the timber, and replant than it received in revenues from the logging companies. Though the federal budget tightened for many nonmilitary programs in the 1980s, subsidy dollars from the taxpayers to the timber industry flowed unabated through that decade and into the budget-conscious 1990s.

By selling timber, the Forest Service nationwide lost $435 million in 1994. This cost the taxpayers $700 per acre logged, according to retired federal timber analyst Robert Wolf's testimony before Congress. During the 1980s, the Forest Service lost $5.6 billion on timber sales. In the Greater Yellowstone Ecosystem alone, including headwaters of the Snake, the government lost $4.9 million from 1992 to 1994 on the national forest timber program. In the Rocky Mountains, each timber job receives a $50,000 taxpayer subsidy through the below-cost sales. Tax money continues to be pumped into the logging program because of the tenacious grip by Western politicians who guard the subsidies while talking a tough line about balancing the federal budget.

In its first year, the Clinton administration proposed a reduction in the worst of the below-cost timber sales, a reform that would have saved taxpayers $274 million during a five-year period and aimed to phase out uneconomic logging. The reform fell to the opposition of congressional

Lodgepole pine forests, such as this one at Redfish Lake, are typical at high elevations. The largest tracts of uncut forest in the United States lie here in central Idaho, but pressures to cut in remaining roadless watersheds are strong.

delegations representing the timber industries. But as the federal budget continues to be ratcheted downward, it's difficult to imagine the subsidized sales escaping scrutiny. In the future, subsidized logging of the public estate might be expected to get at least as much attention as school lunch allowances for low-income children, which came under fire by Republican budget cutters for months in 1995.

Properly organized, conservationists, nonsubsidized timber businesses, and fiscal conservatives can present a daunting challenge to the isolated group of Rocky Mountain congresspeople whose timber subsidy benefits a tiny percentage of the regional, let alone national, population. So far, however, reform efforts have failed in the game of political hardball played by the Western delegation, for whom logging money means big contributions to congressional campaigns. From the late 1980s through early 1990s, the industry's political action committees gave $93,000 to Slade Gorton of Washington, $101,000 to Bob Packwood of

Oregon, and $90,000 to Mark Hatfield. Additional contributions from the industry were likely significant but difficult to identify.

Even when laws stand in the way, elected officials apply unrelenting pressure on Forest Service personnel to "get out the cut." Congressman Larry Craig of Idaho, who received $65,300 from the timber industry, wrote to Forest Service Chief Dale Robertson on May 23, 1991 and called the rate of cutting in Idaho forests a "drastic under-accomplishment." In the letter, which was mysteriously leaked and then published in the Idaho Conservation League's October 1991 newsletter, the Idaho congressman demanded that the chief submit monthly reports to Craig's personal Capitol Hill office, relating agency efforts to speed up the liquidation of Idaho's forests.

For years, the Forest Service supported the subsidized cut by claiming that logging made a healthier forest. Foresters maintained that the maze of expensive, erosion-prone, stream-killing haul roads were not a liability but a benefit that the agency actually *wanted*. As the work of scientists inside the Forest Service caught up with old policy in the 1980s, those views had to be tempered, and in the new political lexicon of the 1990s, the preferred argument for cutting more than the law allowed became one of "salvaging" forests deemed "unhealthy."

REFORM IN BRITISH COLUMBIA

While people grappled with the need to change management of public forests in the United States, British Columbia also launched a program of reform. And reform in that magnificent province, with the greatest expanse of both wild

forest and marketable trees on the continent, had a long way to go.

British Columbia's Rockies, which include the northeastern limits of the Columbia River Basin, form one of the greatest wilderness regions of North America, a wild area larger than anything to the south. Immense expanses of dusky green conifers blanket Kootenay and Yoho National Parks, the Selkirk Mountains of Glacier and Mount Revelstoke National Parks, the Purcell Wilderness Conservancy, and isolated wild valleys. But those forests have become the exception in the southern half of the province, where the timber industry makes American logging look like a small-town lumberyard.

In 1987, 30 percent more timber was cut in the 1,200-mile-long province than in the entire United States National Forest System. On land owned by the provincial government—90 percent of the total—loggers worked virtually unregulated through the 1980s with no limits even on the size of clear-cuts or the setbacks from waterways. Unlike the American system of sale-by-sale contracts which is somewhat amenable to policy change, industrial timber companies in Canada had secured long-term agreements, which they regarded as ownership rights. Eight companies have control of 50 percent of the forests, and 70 percent of the logging profits leave the province. Loggers are cutting the celebrated last frontier of the continent at a breakneck pace.

Forests of the Columbia River Basin are readily accessible compared to more remote reaches of B.C., so much of the watershed, excepting parklands, has already been harvested or fragmented by clear-cuts, some of them running nonstop for miles. One remaining area of unprotected old

LEFT: *Aspens provide important winter feed for wildlife in the Rockies. Timber sales on public lands of this region typically cost the government more than they generate; the subsidies keep some loggers employed but result in costly damage to watersheds, streams, and wildlife habitat.*

The Celgar pulp mill near Castlegar, B.C., smokes the sky along the upper Columbia. Through the 1980s, the Canadian forests were being cut at an unsustainable rate to supply sawmills, paper production, and exports.

growth lies in the jewel-like Cummins basin, nineteen miles upstream from Mica Dam. While higher reaches of the Cummins have been protected from logging, officials in 1995 deferred decisions to spare the lower, more forested part of the watershed.

Opposition to unlimited logging has grown in the province's urban centers and also in communities increasingly dependent on recreation and tourism. Groups such as the Outdoor Recreation Council, Western Canada Wilderness Committee, B.C. Environmental Network, and B.C. Wildlife Federation have plunged into issues of forestry. Opposing old-growth logging in coastal areas, Canadian conservationists staged protests, sit-ins, and boycotts, and gained international attention. Adding official weight to citizens' concerns, provincial analysis of timber supply revealed that harvest levels could drop by 15 to 30 percent in the next fifty years and that employment in the industry could drop from 94,000 people to 69,000.

Announcing a new forest code that called for setbacks from streams and other controls in 1994, Premier Mike Harcourt stated, "For decades, our forests have been taken for granted: there has been too much cut and too little put back into the land. The result is an uncertain future, with fewer trees and fewer jobs for British Columbians." Introducing a Forest Renewal Plan, Harcourt added, "We now have an opportunity to replace confrontation with cooperation and begin working together in partnership to renew our forests and create new jobs."

The Forest Renewal Plan increased payments by industry for timber cut on government land and targeted $2 billion to be paid during a five-year period for reinvestment in forests. Revenues from increased stumpage fees will go to reforestation and repair of environmental damage. To protect the most outstanding areas, Harcourt's administration announced a goal of doubling park and wilderness areas to a total of 12 percent of the province. Before his retirement in 1996, the Premier saw protected acreage climb to 10 percent.

Under Harcourt's administration, the Commission on Resources and Environment (CORE) addressed a broad range of resource planning questions. Committed to a consensus process, the Commission called for locally run meetings with representatives of all interests to hammer out plans at the community level. Participating in the town of Golden, realtor Julia Cundliffe acknowledged the problems of trying to gain agreement among widely divergent interests, but said, "The CORE process really made a difference. After meeting together every week for six weeks, many people came around to understand neighbors with different views. It was good for the community."

Plans for the East and West Kootenay Regions, covering all of the upper Columbia watershed, called for twenty-three new park areas, increasing protected acreage from 11 to 15 percent of the region. About 76 percent of the land remains available for sustainable forestry, mining, tourism, and grazing. An additional 9 percent of the land is federally or privately owned. Though new controls on some resource extraction are proposed, incentives for further development were also offered, including a Prospectors' Assistance Program, a Grazing Enhancement Program, promotion of tourism, and job training.

The Western Canada Wilderness Committee criticized the provincial plans for viewing the forest as a tree farm, for not phasing out clearcutting, and for its focus on logging rather than the health of ecosystems. The B.C. Environmental Network argued that ecosystem management should be the main approach rather than management for marketable timber.

Harcourt's successor, Glen Clark, planned to continue the reform effort and to revise the timber sale process so that it favors small companies, which will process more of the lumber locally and employ more people within the logging communities.

THE HEIGHTENED CONFLICT

In both Canada and the United States, thirty years of effort slowly elevated management from cut-and-run to attempts at sustainable use of entire ecosystems. But each push to protect the forests confronted a political system heavily influenced by the forest industry. Efforts in the 1960s led to

passage of the Wilderness Act but failed to halt logging in the Magruder Corridor, which bisected America's largest woodland wilderness in the Salmon and Clearwater basins. In the 1970s, outrage over summit-to-valley clear-cutting in the Bitterroot Mountains of the Clark Fork basin led to the National Forest Management Act and its requirements for plans and sustainable logging, but then political pressures slanted the planning

Logs being rafted through the locks at Keenleyside Dam on the Columbia above Castlegar. British Columbia had few regulations on cutting before the 1990s but has recently begun reform programs.

process toward rapid extraction, and the Forest Service nationwide called for 262,000 miles of new roads, many of them opening up wild acreage. When the Forest Service recommended reduced harvests in the 1980s, elected officials ordered higher cuts through legislative fiat, ignoring not only the work of scientists but also the supply forecasts of foresters. Unable to rescind environmental measures through an open debate on the subject, in 1989 Senator Mark Hatfield introduced a Section 318 rider attached innocuously to a budget bill. This released a billion board feet of timber from court injunctions and exempted 8 billion more from legal appeals, all of it to be logged while ignoring environmental laws. The Hatfield rider did not, however, go so far as to bypass the Endangered Species Act. About one billion board feet were cut under the Section 318 rider, but the Forest Service cancelled some sales because they were so objectionable. With each challenge, conservationists had less forest to save. They slowed the rate of loss, but each time they won in a public, scientific, economic, and political arena, they later lost to political muscling that dismantled reforms.

Capping the list of protection measures, President Clinton's Northwest Forest Plan had stopped logging on two-thirds of the remaining old-growth acreage in western Oregon and Washington in 1994, but the industry once again gutted reform through political subterfuge. Knowing that they couldn't win in court or political debate about old growth, the timber industry sought to undermine the President's Plan through budget bills.

Attached to a 1995 Appropriations Recisions Bill, whose lofty purpose was to trim $16 billion from the federal deficit, the Republican Congress passed an unrelated salvage rider. Senator Slade Gorton of Washington pushed through the provision requiring the Forest Service and Bureau of Land Management to sell timber "notwithstanding any other provision of law." A whole body of statutes that had evolved and withstood the scrutiny of a quarter-century was thus overridden in a bill supposedly dedicated to the popular notion of balancing the federal budget. The dictum made timber cutting immune from a well-established appeals process, court challenge, and executive branch modification. Opponents dubbed the rider "lawless logging."

Ostensibly aimed at burned areas and trees killed by insects, the salvage rider broadly defined salvage as "dead, dying, diseased, or associated trees." Additionally, it required logging of some unburned, undamaged, completely green tracts of timber. Many of these mandated sales had earlier been withdrawn not only because of the Northwest Forest Plan but because of conflicts with the Endangered Species Act. Sixty-two sales of green old growth, earlier included in Senator Hatfield's 1989 rider but never logged because of endangered species conflicts, were now to be cut. While hundreds of millions of public dollars were being spent to save salmon, half of Congress's mandated sales included critical salmon habitat likely to be degraded by subsidized logging.

Directly countervailent to the Recisions Bill's budget-cutting rhetoric, the Gorton directive required that the Forest Service have the timber logged as fast as possible and specifically stated that sales "shall not be precluded because the costs . . . are likely to exceed the revenues derived." Forest Service officials at first estimated that Congress's demands would cost taxpayers $200 million, but The Wilderness Society projected the public cost of the salvage rider at $430 million in corporate giveaways to an industry with runaway profits in 1994. Then in 1996 the General Accounting Office ascertained that the rider would soak taxpayers for $1 billion, canceling out many of the budget cuts that the same Congress so painfully extracted from oft-needy constituencies lacking the lobbying power of the timber companies.

President Clinton vetoed the first Recisions Bill after 30,000 people contacted the White House opposing the salvage rider, but he signed a second one on July 27, 1995, which included unrelated provisions important to the president. Regarding the salvage rider, the new bill merely decreased the time in which the timber industry's exemption from laws would be in effect. Undermining Clinton's own Northwest Forest Plan, the rider ordered the Forest Service to cut 656 million board feet, including 246 million from timber sales that were proposed before the Northwest Forest Plan but stopped by that hard-earned compromise. Journalist Philip Shabecoff called the rider "the most environmentally retrograde law enacted over the past two generations."

Trying to save face and forest values, the president ordered his agencies to require that all logging fully respect the "spirit and letter of environmental laws." But that order was thrown out in court when the industry confronted the administration. An appeals court refused to hear the case. Logging company lawyers argued for 500 million board feet of green timber as salvage sales, and they won.

Conservationists, so recently dissatisfied with the President's Forest Plan, now faced a congressional mandate incredibly worse. Forced back to an acre-by-acre defense, Tim Hermach of the Native Forest Council in Eugene said, "Here we are, back to defending the best of what's left."

Having no legal recourse, activists relaunched the tactics of protest across the woods of the Northwest and hundreds of people were arrested at five major civil disobedience actions in Oregon in 1995; many more followed in 1996. Law enforcement officers arrested former Congressman Jim Jontz and Audubon Society Vice President Brock Evans in southern Oregon for their sit-down blockade of an old-growth logging job.

Oblivious to public pressure or image, industry lawyers asked a judge in Eugene to fine or jail administration officials for not selling more timber, and the threats from congressmen were no less intimidating. In a related timber issue, Alaska's congressional delegation—trying to bully anyone who disagreed—threatened to cut Forest Service Chief Jack Ward Thomas's salary to zero if he didn't increase logging to arguably illegal levels in old growth of the Tongass National Forest.

Forest advocates attacked the rider not only because of its backdoor approach to cutting green and healthy ancient forests, but also because of its disregard for ecological process and the role of fire. Far from the purported cleanup of charred acreage, typical logging after fires results in soil compaction and erosion, loss of snags and logs needed for nest and den cavities, loss of large woody debris important to land and stream ecology, disturbance of soil microbes essential to the upcoming forest, and construction of roads—the greatest source of soil loss and stream sedimentation. Oblivious to all this, Senator Larry Craig defended the rider by saying that without logging, "there will be no value. It will have rotted away."

One of the worst problems with the rider and perhaps the biggest reason it passed was that it would open up untouched watersheds in Idaho and Montana never before logged. These roadless areas would then lose their eligibility as protected wilderness, allowing yet more logging. In this way, congressmen circumvented restrictions in potential wilderness areas, something they had not been able to do through an open debate about wilderness in the northern Rockies.

Most egregious on a long list of sales, timber in the South Fork Salmon basin of Idaho was put up for bid, an action viewed by fisheries experts as a return to the Dark Ages. Once the richest of all salmon habitat, whole windrows of spawning redds once blanketed the gravelly streambed. That all ended when logging caused blowouts of landslides silting over the gravel beds in 1964. Through a thirty-year recovery period, this legendary salmon stream was mending toward its old richness.

Part of the South Fork basin burned, and in 1996 the Thunderbolt sale included 3,237 acres for logging, complete with new roads and the likelihood of disaster once again. Soil scientists ranked a third of the area as prone to landslides; two-thirds was roadless. The National Marine Fisheries Service opposed the sale because it would jeopardize the salmon; Regional Director William Stelle said, "Issues of common sense and fact went right out the window on this one." Other critics included the Environmental Protection Agency, which called the sale "environmentally unacceptable." The Idaho Department of Fish and Game, Inter-Tribal Fish Commission, and entire conservation community opposed the

logging. A peer review by fisheries biologists flunked the proposal. The Forest Service's own biologist said the sale was justified by circular reasoning, incorrect scientific procedure, and illogical statements.

To all this criticism the Forest Service posed the creative rebuttal that the sale would generate money to solve erosion problems caused by logging thirty years ago; now they could finally put gravel on the old roads to reduce erosion. The Forest Service silenced the battery of agencies opposing it and pushed to sell the burned timber under the implicit or explicit congressional threat of budget cuts.

No logging companies matched the already-subsidized minimum bid, so the Forest Service put the Thunderbolt sale up again and finally sold the timber for half its advertised value. Boise Cascade bought it, but not without arguing to weaken conservation requirements. Having received $15,000 from Boise Cascade in campaign contributions, Senator Larry Craig ignored the findings of every fishery agency and criticized the Environmental Protection Agency for opposing the sale. For a million dollars' worth of timber, Thunderbolt could lose the government up to $2.8 million, not counting new damage to be inflicted on the South Fork of the Salmon.

Another controversial sale would open up the Middle Fork of the Flathead River basin in Montana near one of the West's great wild and scenic rivers, including prime grizzly bear habitat one mile from Glacier National Park. Yet another Columbia Basin salvage sale, at Thunder Mountain in northcentral Washington, lay in the state's largest remaining forested, roadless area. The Northwest Ecosystem Alliance bid the highest price for the timber but the Forest Service refused to award the contract because the Alliance did not intend to cut the trees. Costing the government $300,000, the Thunder Mountain sale was sold to the second-highest bidder for $28,000. Finally responding to public outrage at the salvage rider's scope, Secretary of Agriculture Dan Glickman, in 1996, announced a new policy to prohibit salvage logging in most roadless areas and to limit sales of green timber under the salvage umbrella.

Almost as soon as the salvage rider had passed, with its two-year duration limit, Idaho's Senator Craig went to work on a long-term salvage law to continue sales under the ruse of "forest health." Craig called his bill the Federal Lands Forest Health Protection and Restoration Act, but in a curious strategy for health, protection, and restoration, it mandated that environmental laws be waived; that scientific guidance be bypassed; that citizen involvement and appeals be restricted; and that logging be increased. Though a vociferous balanced budget advocate, Craig set no limit on government deficits in order to allow logging. The Congressional Research Service estimated that this new "forest health" bill would cost $50 million over revenues.

Representing The Wilderness Society in Boise, Craig Gehrke said, "Senator Craig's bill states that to save a forest you have to cut it down." In 1995, Arthur Partridge, professor of Forest Disease and Insect Problems at the University of Idaho, testified to Congress that the forest "health crisis" was a hoax. After studying the forests in the northern Rockies, he reported, "We detected the lowest levels of disease and insect activity in twenty-eight years." Leaving no logging stone unturned, Senator Craig tried unsuccessfully to attach an amendment to yet another budget bill that would have waived the Forest Service's established harvest limits in the Clearwater National Forest.

Taking an opposite view, in 1995 Oregon Democrat Elizabeth Furse introduced a bill to totally rescind the current salvage rider. In 1996 she nearly passed the measure, but lost by two votes in the Republican House.

Bills such as the salvage rider will continue to be proposed, and what counts for the Columbia Basin forests are elections. The fate of the forest depends on whether people support the Larry Craigs of the world or candidates who agree with Elizabeth Furse.

As if calling clear-cutting of federal forests "restoration" and ordering federal agencies to sell timber at a loss to taxpayers were not enough, some Western politicians sought to undo conservation efforts as old as Republican Teddy Roosevelt's presidency by arguing for state takeover of federal forest land. Republican congressional members pushed to deed Forest Service and Bureau of Land Management acreage to states or to establish joint management responsibilities. This latter arrangement could provide their constituent industries with the ability to collect federal subsidies while extracting trees, water, and minerals without federal restrictions, which is to say, without any restrictions at all in many cases. These proposals were a thinly disguised land grab for those who want to log and mine without federal intervention and especially without consideration for the Endangered Species Act. From a district near the national jewel of Mount Rainier in Washington, a staff member for Representative Linda Smith said, "Why should someone in D. C. be telling us how

Old growth at Opal Creek still stands thanks to the diligence of conservationists working to save the small amount of original forest that remains in the Northwest.

to manage our land? Linda thinks parks can remain a national legacy under state control." The state under discussion had just passed the most extreme "takings" bill in the nation, requiring local and state government to pay developers to comply with the most basic of long-standing laws. Republican House member Wes Cooley of Oregon—before he was caught misrepresenting his military and academic experience—introduced legislation for a state takings of three million acres of Bureau of Land Management property belonging to all Americans.

State control would usually loosen restrictions on extraction and development of public land. For example, the U.S. Forest Service often protects one hundred feet on either side of streams for wildlife while the Oregon State Forest Practices Act allows logging right up to the water simply if fish in the stream are less than six inches long. In 1996 the Oregon legislature sought a wholesale reduction in environmental controls and offered some insight about what to expect with the proposed state takeover of federal public land. Journalist Molly Dee Anderson reported that under state laws, allowable logging in old-growth forests would double, which means only a token of the remaining token would be left—most of it in already designated national parks and wilderness areas.

After a decade of hopeful efforts at reform, the pressures on the forests of the Columbia Basin were the worst they had been since the days of the robber barons of the early 1900s, who took whatever they wanted without legal or moral restraint.

THE WINDS OF CHANGE

Returning to the Columbia forests I first visited in 1967, I traveled to Opal Creek in the central Cascades of Oregon, which remains the way old-growth forests have been for the millennia. Cathedral groves of fir and cedar climb the slopes above the Little North Santiam River and its opal-tinted tributary. The hush of the forest and the shafts of sunlight beaming through moss-cloaked foliage give an air of the sacred. Thousands of people who stroll on the trails here each year sense what the ancient forests of the western Cascades were once really like. This woodland is considered to be the largest unlogged watershed in Oregon.

Threatened for decades by logging proposals and still coveted by timber companies anxious to cut the last unprotected stands of ancient trees, Opal Creek may be the subject of the longest-running tree war in the West. Held at bay by the dogged efforts of local resident George Atiyeh, the Friends of Opal Creek, and an army of forest enthusiasts, each proposal to log was halted. Yet each proposal to forever protect the 36,000-acre tract of the original Oregon was also stopped.

The future of Opal Creek may yet be secured as a heritage of lasting value, saved by people who appreciate the best of the original Northwest. Elsewhere, the fate of forests in the Columbia Basin lies in the hands of voters and the winds of political change, from the Rockies to the Pacific.

CHAPTER FOUR

THE VALUE OF LAND

A Troubling Forecast

The wild salmon have almost been lost, and the old-growth forest has been cut to a remnant, but the land remains, rock solid and durable. The timeless views of Mount Jefferson and the Lost River Range, of green gorges and sagebrush plains, of Okanagan orchards and Sauvie Island farms all offer hope that a changing society in the Columbia River Basin can do better than it has so far. The way that all these lands are developed, today, will tell much about the future of the watershed and its value to coming generations.

When I think of land use changes, I first think of Jackson, Wyoming, at the headwaters of the Snake River, the Columbia Basin's highest major town in elevation. On my first trip there, hitchhiking in 1969, I was fascinated by that enclave in the mountains— the sweep of the valley, the velvet of meadows, the big-sky open space for which the West is known, and the uncluttered clarity of it all. Haystacks resembling giant bread loaves dotted a valley that seemed to

LEFT: *The rural and agricultural land of the Yakima watershed is undergoing rapid change with increasing urbanization.*

have escaped the twentieth century, and the high-ways curved lightly on the countryside until almost within the twenty-block town of Jackson.

Today, a roadside strip with K-Mart and Denny's fills the southern approach, a strip that could almost be photocopied from suburban Idaho Falls or worse, from Highway 2 in Spokane—the Basin's ultimate commercial-strip city. Subdivisions curl from the main roads with new homes that seem to pop up in the fields overnight. But mainly it is on the west side of the Snake River where the valley called Jackson Hole has been so noticably transformed. The changeover was ignited by a world-class ski resort started in the 1960s and fueled by a commercial jetport within Grand Teton National Park itself, where dozens of planes daily land and take off, 737s framed as if for TV ads in America's most famous mountain view. The real estate industry flourished, and west bank ranchland was lopped off for million and multimillion dollar houses, entire cul-de-sacs of them on pastures, meadows, wetlands, forestland, floodplains, buttes, and even the flank of the Teton Range itself, all of it once habitat for elk, deer, bears, antelope, beavers, moose, and buffalo. The average new home in Jackson Hole sells for $500,000. The average local wage is $22,000.

The ultimate irony is that the west side of the valley is *lower* than the Snake River, which runs down the valley's center. Some of the west side is *twenty feet* lower, and drops more whenever there's an earthquake. Only a rock-fill levee holds the river on course and delays its inexorable slide, tugged by gravity, to the western limits of Jackson Hole. Lowlands west of the levee were once zoned as floodplain to limit new building, but

developers cooked the numbers dealing with flood risk, regarded the levee as invincible, and worked the angles until they convinced the county commissioners to change the zoning, despite the advice of the county's expert hydrologist, Dr. Luna Leopold. Now the thin armor of levee keeps the floodwater and the river's migration away from some of the Columbia Basin's wealthiest neighborhoods but that levee is in the second most seismically active zone in America where a map of faults looks like a broken eggshell.

All the development running roughshod over the natural landscape outraged a lot of people and gave rise to one of the most active environmental constituencies in the Rocky Mountains. The Jackson Hole Alliance for Responsible Planning is the largest membership group in the area, the Jackson Hole Land Trust acquires easements for open space, and county voters have supported more progressive commissioners than can be found elsewhere in the mountain states. But the pull of natural beauty is like that of a siren, and the push for development is powerful, influential, and charged with money. Growth has been moderated but not contained.

A county land use plan, even with progressive measures for wildlife and scenery, still allows a population of 17,000 to swell to 40,000—almost the size of nearby Idaho Falls, which is Idaho's third largest city. At that point we can expect to see nearly two-and-a-half times the amount of everything man-made that we now see in Jackson—two-and-a-half times the garbage, the overhead wires, the police cars, the jet aircraft, the grocery store lines, and the yard lights that dim the stars at night. The presumption is that the county plan will then be modified to accommodate yet more growth. A hopeful sign of the times occurred in 1996, when, by a landslide, voters rejected a business-sponsored initiative to reinstate a "bed" tax on tourists that would have been used for a multimillion-dollar promotion campaign to generate even more tourism.

Seeing the changes near Jackson, Bend, Whitefish, and dozens of other once-idyllic towns in the Columbia Basin makes me think of a question I heard years ago: why is it that when we destroy something people have made it's called vandalism, and when we destroy something God has made, it's called development? We all need some development—at least a place to live. But for each community, how much is enough, and what can be done to lessen our weight on the land?

The development in the Columbia Basin isn't all as discordant as the commercial strip on the southern approach to Jackson. Many of the towns, farms, and ranches of the Rockies and Northwest lie on the ground as if they fit and belong there. The roll of cultivated fields and fence lines in the White Salmon Valley of southern Washington, the home and garden neighborhoods of Nelson, British Columbia, and even Portland with its classic stone architecture, waterfall fountains, and downtown as beautiful as any big city in America are just three among hundreds of scenes showing how people have settled with style and a sense of belonging. But much of the development happening today is different. It breaks the fundamental but elusive rule of harmony between environment and investment.

And there has been more development than ever before—far more. In the 1990s, the region boomed as no other in America. With the rush to the Northwest, the cities became clogged with growth, the small towns were ringed with drive-in strips, and the countryside, where farms, wildlife, and purely exultant space so recently pleased the eye, was chopped up for lots. Rather than a ribbon of road laid down to take us from one place to another, pavement becomes a whole class of landscape, smearing out beyond curbs in a free-form expanse of parking lots and shopping centers. Homesites are sown as the final crop on rich farms where the durable land is suddenly a perishable commodity. Urban development takes away 75,000 acres of forest every year in Oregon and Washington—more than logging takes on federal land. In the four-state region of Washington, Oregon, Montana, and Idaho, population grew 48 percent from 1969 to 1993 while the national average was 28 percent. "All towns, including Los Angeles, say they need more economic development," said Andy Kerr of the Oregon Natural Resources Council. "In our region, that goes for places as large as Portland and as small as Joseph. When is there enough?" None of the towns admit they want to be like the next one up, but they do everything they can to get there. With each acre of new pavement, with every thousand or hundred thousand new immigrants, this region more resembles urban California, and the chance of sustaining the native landscape that has nurtured people for so long is fading away.

In 1995 alone, Washington grew by 95,950 people, with 60 percent of the increase owing to in-migration. Development in the Columbia Basin of eastern Washington outpaced the Puget Sound side on a percentage basis and represented one-third of state growth. From 1990 to 1994, Oregon's population increased by 60,000 a year;

about 71 percent were in-migrants from other states and countries. From 1989 to 1995, Idaho was the fastest growing state in the region on a percentage basis and for a while was one of the fastest growing states in the nation.

In 1995 the Northwest Power Planning Council forecast that population in the four-state region (an area larger than the Columbia Basin and including Seattle) will climb from 9.7 to 15.7 million by the year 2015 in a high growth scenario, which is likely if recent years are any indication. A medium-range projection calls for 2.8 million more people during the twenty-year period ending in 2015. Under this forecast, Washington is expected to increase from 5.3 to 6.8 million; Oregon from 3.9 to 4.8 million; Idaho from 1.1 to 1.5 million; and western Montana from 329,000 to 379,000. Nearly all of Idaho's population lives in the Columbia Basin while 82 percent of Oregonians and 22 percent of Washingtonians reside there. The entire province of British Columbia is expected to double from its current 3.8 million people to 7.5 by the year 2030.

It's easy to see why people want to come. A number of studies identified quality of life as the main reason. Availability of jobs is important, but a revealing report, *Economic Well-Being and Environmental Protection in the Pacific Northwest,* written by thirty Northwest economists, credited much of the new job growth to quality of life. Can people come without ruining what attracted them? Can communities avoid the plague of urban and suburban ills that drove the newcomers to leave wherever they were? Will there someday be an end to the pressure for growth and change, or will it continue indefinitely? Wondering about all this, I first visited the communities of central Washington, separated from the big Northwestern cities by the Cascade Range.

REVAMPING KITTITAS VALLEY

Beginning at the summit of Snoqualmie Pass, east of Seattle, the Yakima River headwaters drop eastward. The 6,000-square-mile watershed is the largest river basin in Washington next to the Columbia, which the Yakima enters near the Tri-Cities. The picturesque upper valley spreads out from its river bottom, where a cottonwood corridor adjoins the grasslands and hills. Conifers on north-facing slopes fade away in lower elevations. The rolling, ash-fertile flanks of the Cascades tier down to desert where the sun shines three hundred days a year and snow-charged tributaries swirl in meanders above a twenty-six-mile-long canyon separating the upper Yakima's Kittitas Valley from the lower Yakima Valley. Long a refuge from the urban, rainy west side of the state, the Kittitas Valley now lies on the main line of Interstate 90, and travelers ramp off with ease after driving two hours or less from Seattle.

"The valley's filling up," said Clayton Denman, a Central Washington University anthropology professor. "People come for a lot of reasons, but the push is greater than the pull," he said, referring to the drive to escape the Puget Sound chain of cities. In 1970 Denman founded the Small Towns Institute, dedicated to protecting small-town values across America, values becoming endangered in his own hometown of Ellensburg and elsewhere in the basin. The "filling up" is evident in summer along the transparent Cle Elum River, a Yakima tributary where 6,000 campers move in on weekends. New vacation cabins sprout up and old cabins are leveled to make room for $300,000 homes. The baronistic Plum Creek Timber Company sells off parcels once it clear-cuts them. "We studied one section in the Yakima's rural headwaters," said geographer Morris Uebelacker of Central Washington University, "and it's been divided into 650 private parcels. Seventeen governmental entities make decisions about that land. Even the birds don't know what to do."

In 1991, the state Office of Financial Management released its year-2010 growth projections for Kittitas County. The projections were reached by 1995—fifteen years early in a time frame of only nineteen years. Population similarly surged in the 1970s, then tapered off, though county planner Debbie Randall expected no such lull this time. "We're so close to the Seattle area," she said, "and people are looking for property." Department of Transportation data indicated that 500 commuters make the Seattle drive, spending four hours daily in their cars. Property costs have climbed to west-side rates.

Randall pointed out that so far, only one in a hundred created lots has been built on; while the picture is already looking different, the real change in the pastoral valley is yet to come. When the zoning was being drawn up, lot size proposals for agricultural districts ranged from one acre to eighty acres. Local officials compromised on twenty acres but riddled the regulation with loopholes. Once created, the lot can be subdivided one more time, presumably for a child in the family but in fact, for anyone. The upshot is that big residential lots quilt the windy flats, and agriculture seldom survives in the agricultural zones. "We have a lot of houses surrounded by weeds," Randall explained. And the weeds are not

native forbs and wildflowers; they are noxious exotics such as knapweed and cheat grass, which invade overgrazed or otherwise disturbed landscapes and pose a plague to cattle, wildlife, and people alike.

Kittitas County enrolled in the federal flood insurance program, which requires a modicum of floodplain regulation in order to qualify for subsidized insurance, which, in turn, is required for a federally-backed mortgage issued to anyone building on land likely to flood. Overtaken by a rabid private property rights movement with an anti-government gospel of "I own my land and can do whatever I want," the county rescinded the floodplain regulations and hence the flood insurance program in the early 1980s. Harassed by people who then could not get mortgages because they lacked the federally-backed insurance, and pushed by banks that profit from the mortgages, the county reentered the program, but halfheartedly. It granted permits without proper restrictions, in effect reaping the federal subsidy of insurance without upholding the local end of the bargain. Yet the same "property rights" advocates will typically expect federal disaster aid when the next flood wipes out new development on sites where damage could have been avoided. The county was placed on probation by the Federal Emergency Management Agency.

In a wave of responsibility and forethought, Kittitas County in 1990 joined the state's Growth Management Program even though, as a rural county, officials didn't have to participate. The state program required that basic guidelines of good planning be met. When real estate interests recaptured local government, a rerun of the flood insurance fiasco ensued and the county tried to back out of the growth management program, but it couldn't. The state requires that the county show it can actually accommodate and pay for the growth it allows, but brakes of any kind are scarcely applied in this climate of rapid buying and selling, wheeling and dealing.

With similar dynamics of growth and subdivision, Chelan County commissioners, north of Kittitas, refused to meet guidelines of the state law. After the county had accepted and spent $500,000 in state aid to meet its planning obligations, Washington Governor Mike Lowry had to notify local officials that, under state law, $1.6 million in state aid for road maintenance to the county would have to be cut.

Morris Uebelacker said, "An old Indian friend of mine once told me that you have to stay in a place for five generations to know it. So don't be surprised if you feel confused after you've just arrived in a valley changing as rapidly as this is." The geographer is the fourth-generation Uebelacker here. "What I know from my uncles is that this place is trashed from what it was. I call it stepping down the biomass pyramid. First they wiped out the large animals. Now we've done the same to trees. The big ponderosa are gone. The stability is knocked out of the system, and it becomes simpler and simpler, less productive, less resistant, until we have a desert and monoculture of exotic weeds where we used to have a pine savanna and grassland full of animals and people living in relative balance."

Ken Hammond, chairman of the Geography Department at Central Washington University, said, "People come here because it's a nice place to live. It *is* a nice place to live, but it won't be for long. We're on the road of Napa Valley in California; it

was a nice place, but few people would say it is today. Twenty acres here, twenty acres there—the cumulative effect is staggering. Soon, only the wealthy will be able to buy land or live here.

"For a time, I was not so discouraged. In the late 1970s there was a genuine effort to enact good zoning. But then the price got to be too much. In forty years of this work, I've noticed that it's very rare to get a local government decision that's long-term in its view. Property values went up, the real estate and development stakes escalated, and people can be bought, can't they?"

Taking a more hopeful outlook, as she must in order to do her job, planner Debbie Randall noted that when the county violated flood insurance rules, only one planner was employed. "Now we have six, and can give more attention to the jobs we have to do. Six years ago, the Planning Department gave administrative variances to a rule for a hundred-foot setback from streams, but now a hearing is held and variances given only if the owner has no place else to build."

Yet, as geographer Hammond pointed out, the floodplain was being filled for a golf course, and rampaging high water in February 1996 had barely subsided before people began to rebuild on the same damage-prone sites. While the antigovernment rhetoric was repeated *ad infinitum* in 1996, county officials accepted $4.9 million of federal funds for flood disaster aid, much of the need owing to a lack of willingness to effectively regulate the floodplain. Then, instead of relocating low-lying homes, residents agitated for more taxpayer dollars to construct levees. These encourage more development, which will someday be threatened by higher floods and resulting levee failures, such as those on the Mississippi River in 1993, in the Sacramento Valley in 1986, and in other cases nationwide.

The solution to the land use problems of Kittitas Valley requires no new knowledge, no legal breakthrough, and no new government program. It requires little sacrifice on the part of people living in Kittitas Valley or emigrating there, and it requires very little money. The solution is to simply elect public-spirited people to local office. Using existing programs, they could then plan for a better future. But, acknowledging a strong resistance in the county to better land use controls, Hammond said, "Our strong property rights advocates see themselves only as oppressed taxpayers and not as citizens; they admit to no responsibilities to the larger community. That seems to be the tenor of the times and I doubt that it will change soon enough to allow salvation for the Kittitas Valley."

The Future of Yakima

To go from Ellensburg to Yakima, you can drive over Umtanum Ridge on the Interstate or wind through the Yakima River Canyon, which I did this time, emerging at the edge of the largest urban area on the east slope of the Cascades. Rural development is scattered out in bungalows, ranch houses, and mobile homes from busy suburban strips and a downtown core that describes a small city, not a large town. The county housed 207,600 people in 1996, and 260,000 are expected by 2015.

The Yakama Indians, now on a reservation south of the city, had thrived here on salmon and a fruitful land. Then irrigation brought the growing settlement of white people. Along 175 miles

of river, half a million acres are now ditched and sprinkled by the Yakima Project of the Federal Bureau of Reclamation, which, with federal funds, built six storage dams and five diversion dams. These large waterworks coupled with two hundred frost-free days a year set the county's stage for an agricultural economy ranking sixteenth in America. Apples, hops, and cattle are big crops. Farmers depend heavily on Mexican labor; much of the county's population growth and a great majority of new school students are Mexican. While farmworkers used to migrate through during the harvesting season, many now stay year round. County Planning Director Dick Anderwald said, "Many people feel threatened by the level of immigration from Mexico, but others see it as an opportunity, similar to when people from Oklahoma and the Midwest came here in the 1930s. Perhaps our biggest challenge is in dealing with the ever-increasing cultural diversity in the community."

Commercial strip development is affecting virtually every community in the Columbia Basin. Here at the edge of Ellensburg, the conversion of rural land is evident.

New housing goes up on the hills of Yakima. Erosion on steep slopes, building on the flood plains, and filling of wetlands are a result of suburban growth but can be avoided through zoning that saves tax dollars and protects existing property values.

Yakima has the highest crime rate in the state and twenty-fourth highest in the nation. In 1994, 120 offenses occurred for every 1,000 people, and gang activity is growing. Centered in the mostly rural Columbia River Basin where one might assume insulation from urban problems, the city became a hub of drug distribution in the 1980s. Much of the contraband is imported by Mexicans passing as farmworkers. When the community decided to aggressively attack the problem, Yakima gained nationwide notoriety as a community that would not allow itself to be overrun by drug lords. Local officials succeeded in having a federal office established to combat drug distribution.

Yakima also has a nearby mountain playground that includes the exquisite Mount Rainier—one of the highlights of the National Park System—only seventy miles away. Within the community, a riverfront is being reclaimed as parkland with a bikeway, playgrounds, and open space. In a creative and quirky solution to meeting budget needs in the postgovernment era, the nonprofit Yakima Greenway Foundation operates a $400,000-a-year bingo parlor as the way to fund the riverfront park.

The area accommodates two extremes of housing. The county planner explained, "We are seeing tremendous growth in high-end homes. Millions of dollars are being spent by children of the early agricultural industrialists, and by the wealthy who sell their houses in Seattle or California and reinvest in large homes to avoid capital gains taxes." Gated communities of new mansions with carpet-perfect Chem-lawns are appearing on the arid hills above the city. "In contrast, older, close-in neighborhoods have one-family houses with four families living in them and portable toilets in the backyard." Unable to find shelter, itinerant men live under the Yakima River bridges and compete with summer campers for tent sites in the canyon.

A pattern of subdividing farmland was well established before the first county plan in 1974. By 1982, zoning sought to protect agricultural use with forty-acre-minimum lot sizes. But a loophole, which planner Anderwald would like to close, allows farmers to sell one lot every five years, leading to a landscape dotted with homes and half-acre horse pastures, perhaps worse for its piecemeal approach than well-planned developments consuming less space overall.

Following guidelines required by the state's Growth Management Act, the county regulates critical areas such as floodplains, wetlands, and steep slopes. While the regulations no doubt help, you can still see encroachments into the flood zone and homes notched into hillsides that look as if they will liquefy in one good spring freshet.

Seasoned by years in the political minefields of land use planning, Anderwald believes that support for his program is not fading but growing among the general population. "It's now easier to do good planning than it used to be," he said. "We have an increasing constituency that has seen the ravages of growth elsewhere. They're more aware. I know of a designer of video covers from Los Angeles who decided he'd rather live here. He's not in the Yellow Pages, but he might make $250,000 a year conducting his business from afar, thanks to modern technology. He's a potential supporter of planning, and he's typical of people who now speak up in land use controversies. It used to be that neighbors supported proposed zoning changes—whatever anyone wanted to do—but now they're often critical. There's an interest in keeping the qualities that drew people here in the first place." To cope with the pressure of change, the planner would like to see tighter limits on development in agriculture zones, protection of wetlands, and clustering of new development to protect rural acreage, thus maintaining a rural way of life.

With a growing population, conflicts increase. Looking at the problems of both Yakima and Kittitas Counties, and striving in a distinctive way to face the future, the Yakima River Watershed Council has brought people of many interests together. Mel Wagner, director of this consensus-based group of fifty, said, "We've got every kind of problem you can imagine, but we're doing a watershed plan, and we have the will to solve our problems. Ten years ago nobody would have thought it possible that irrigators, environmentalists, Indians, fishermen, and developers could do this."

With its genesis in the parched year of 1993, the Council seeks to bring people together to consider the whole of watershed management. "The big irrigators tried to get increased storage at Bumping Reservoir on a Yakima tributary, but they were shot down," Wagner said. "Their only hope was to work with people and find consensus. All parties had to be participants, including the Yakama Indian Nation.

"For years, the river had been treated like a big irrigation ditch and the flows cut below 300 cubic feet per second. Over time, people began to recognize other values. One is recreation. Another is fish and biological values. The Yakama Nation wants better instream flows for salmon and also more irrigation. People participate because their voices are heard. They're heard because we need them." Similar efforts to work together are proliferating in the West, but not without concern that so-called cooperative approaches will favor those who have the most power, giving them an easy forum to push their agenda. But Wagner remains optimistic.

"There's now tremendous enthusiasm that this can work. The different sides are beginning to understand each other. There's a centralizing force to keep people in a process based on logic, fairness, and equity. Very few of the interests are selfish. It's not selfish to protect your livelihood. It's not selfish to want clean, healthy water. The nature of water is universal; we all care about it. We're finding that we can work together for these things."

Here along the Yakima, or anywhere else people try to work out their differences, everybody has to recognize that the time has come for change. And to break out of old, gridlocked modes of operation, the control of the future

RIGHT: *Ukiah, in the drylands of northeastern Oregon, remains much the way it has been for years, but new development crowds many of the communities and rural landscapes throughout the Columbia Basin.*

communities as well as water for farming."

With organizations such as the Yakima River Watershed Council, people are seeking new paths to the future and grappling with the problems and conflicts of change. Perhaps that seed of interest will grow to include the use of land, the impending scarcity of open space, and the need for healthy communities.

A UNIVERSAL EXPERIENCE

Virtually every town in the Columbia Basin feels land development pressures in one way or another. In British Columbia, the small-town appeal and natural environment attract new residents. Golden is a logging town evolving with a new economy. Revelstoke combines recreation and industry. Nakusp lies perfectly sited on the shores of Upper Arrow Lake. Nelson, along the dammed-up Kootenay, is a favorite destination of Canadians seeking small-town life and amenities. The Okanagan Valley towns of Kelowna, Penticton, and Osoyoos bustle with a warm, dry climate and thriving economy closer to the Vancouver urban area. While an urban exodus from cities to small towns has characterized the American West since the mid-1980s, that trend is just starting in B.C. with West Coast urbanites buying property in the Kootenay region.

In Idaho, land development in the 1990s reached virtual boomtown proportions. The state drew new employers and residents with aggressive economic policies and a reputation for low crime, quality of life, and a natural environment, all of which people elsewhere desperately sought. But with the new development, Idaho communities are changing. "The new construction and

ABOVE: *New development affects the Columbia Basin from its largest cities to its quietest countrysides. Even Stanley, Idaho, feels the pressures for growth.*

cannot lie with any single group. Recognizing these points, Wagner continued, "More residents are coming into the area, and they learn that 85 percent of the water is used for agriculture. They want good drinking water, and they don't accept the old assumptions. They realize that water has a public value. People are now interested in livable congestion remind me of Denver in its boom years, decades ago," said Hugh Harper, a longtime Boise resident. In 1993, Harper had to move away from Boise because the city's air quality had deteriorated so much. Winter temperature inversions trap car exhaust and smoke in the valley lying against the Boise Front of the Rocky Mountains; once a garden scene, it is now shrouded in smog. In 1995, violent crime in Idaho was up 10 percent, drug offenses grew by 52 percent, and robberies increased 22 percent above the year before.

A Boise businessman and U.S. Senate candidate in 1996, Walt Minnick recognized, "Excessive growth is what drives the other problems. Because of our quality of life, Idaho is an appealing place to the new footloose industries. But with our existing tax structure, growth never has paid its own way. Now we're outrunning our abilities to maintain the very attributes that caused the region to be attractive. In the Northern Rockies we're still falling over ourselves begging industries to come to our rapidly growing cities. It's like throwing gas on a fire."

In the same year, with a different attitude, Republican Governor Phil Batt said, "A good bit of Idaho will benefit from new growth. We don't have a lot of choice; we have to accommodate it."

Total value of all construction in Idaho tripled between 1988 and 1995 with records set every year for nine years. In 1994, a record 23,000 people moved to Idaho. Planning programs in some counties grapple with the pace of change, but most attempts fail to challenge the economic pressures and a deeply ingrained attitude opposing government regulation—even regulation aimed at maintaining traditional values. When it's obvious

that crime, taxes, congestion, and housing prices climb hand in hand with the growth rate, many people still show little willingness to come to terms with their future. Even in the Ketchum-Hailey area where environmental interest runs higher than elsewhere in the state, poorly regulated development has allowed floodplain homesites along the Wood River, and new building crowds scenic highway corridors of the valley. A condo complex took the place of winter elk range and left behind nothing but the name: Elkhorn. Quiet ranch towns to the south are beginning to suburbanize as bedroom communities—the only places where people on workers' wages can afford to live.

SAVING THE GORGE

Taking a unique approach to the loss of open space in one of the Basin's most extraordinary landscapes, supporters of the Columbia River Gorge in Washington and Oregon succeeded in getting federal legislation passed in 1986 after years of strenuous effort and compromise. Addressing a patchwork of private and national forestland between The Dalles and Troutdale (just east of Portland), the legislation created a Columbia River Gorge Commission made up of six members appointed by the governors and six from the counties. The goal of the program is to protect scenic and other natural resources and encourage growth in existing towns. Under the federal legislation, the Commission prepared a management plan. Counties are responsible for land use regulations to implement the plan, but if ordinances are not consistent, the Gorge Commission can enforce its own rules. The U.S. Forest Service provides for

recreation, manages its substantial holdings for scenic value, and buys critical parcels of open space if owners are willing to sell. As of 1995, the Forest Service acquired 23,000 acres, but another $20 million was needed from a reluctant Congress to finish buying the most consequential tracts.

Designed for local acceptance, the plan encourages growth in 28,500 acres of urban areas, allows a variety of development on 149,400 acres of private land, and restricts houses to forty acres each on another 114,600 acres. Existing uses are not affected. The Scenic Area is a pioneering case of land protection that recognizes the complexity of the private and public interface and the need to combine local land use regulation, regionwide planning standards, and public acquisition of key parcels.

Lauri Aunin, director of Friends of the Columbia River Gorge, said, "People now *expect* the Gorge to be protected. They think it *is* protected. But we have a long way to go. The Gorge is amazingly fragile and special, and land development is still the biggest threat." Clark County, Washington, has a population of 267,000 and is expected to grow to 346,000 by 2010. "Though most of that growth lies outside the boundary, the Gorge is affected by what happens nearby," Aunin said. Regarding the entire Gorge, she added, "If we build out to the existing regulations even under the management plan, there will be a loss of open-space values."

Notwithstanding the plan's concessions to local development interests, a property rights backlash put the Commission under constant siege, with disgruntled landowners erecting billboards accusing the federal government of a land grab. Skamania County, Washington, gained more people between 1990 and 1994 than it did in the entire decade of the 1980s, and its city of Washougal lobbied Congress to open the Gorge to uncontrolled sprawl. The county reluctantly adopted a plan, though it included a proposal for variances from Gorge Commission standards, which would effectively nullify the whole program.

The fight to hold onto the gains of 1986 promises to be a protracted battle for Friends of the Columbia River Gorge and other supporters of this remarkable corridor at the doorstep of Portland. "It's difficult to overcome the kinds of development pressures that are encroaching on the Gorge," Lauri Aunin said, "but a lot of people have the will to try. People who have been living in the Gorge and new people moving in are concerned about the quality of life. Once they're aware of the problems, we hope they will act."

THE OREGON WAY

The ultimate growth site in the Columbia watershed is Portland, where 28 percent of the Basin-wide population lives. Slow growth in the 1980s gave way like a broken dam to 35,000 newcomers a year in the 1990s, with no end in sight. The four-county area is expected to grow from 1.7 million people in 1995 to 2.3 million in 2020. Analysts for the *Oregonian* estimated that the public facilities needed for the growth, including roads, water, sewers, and parks, will cost $15.8 billion over the next twenty years, or $28,500 per new home. Not even reflecting those public costs, the price of houses jumped 32 percent between 1991 and 1995 while median income rose 8 percent, leaving many local families priced out of home-buying ability.

Growth in Portland and all of the state's municipalities is affected by one of the most effective land use laws passed at the state level in America. As the first of ten states achieving some success in grappling with land use issues, Oregon enacted pathbreaking legislation in 1973 to create the Land Conservation and Development Commission. The Commission reviews plans of the 278 local governments and assures that each satisfies nineteen state goals. The principal requirement is establishment of a growth boundary, inside of which development is encouraged and outside of which open space remains lightly settled.

The state Commission and other reviewers

LEFT: *The natural beauty of the Columbia River Gorge motivated people to seek new ways of accommodating urban growth without sacrificing the splendor of open space. The Gorge legislation, however, is under constant siege.*

have reported that the program cuts the high public costs of sprawl, eliminates red tape by efficiently approving developments that qualify, allows for a variety of affordable housing, and saves open space. With broad-based support, the state law was instigated by farmer and legislator Hector Mcpherson and still enjoys solid support of the Farm Bureau in an unusual alliance with environmentalists. The land use act has withstood three developer-sponsored statewide initiatives aimed at weakening or eliminating the program.

"The law has worked," said Christine Cook of 1000 Friends of Oregon, a group dedicated to watchdogging the effort. "The urban growth boundary is evident in many places where the towns end and the countryside begins. The land use code has the reputation as the law that keeps Oregon a hospitable and pleasant place."

In the fall of 1995, the Portland Metro Government Council heard overwhelming opposition to expansion of growth boundaries. In a poll taken by the *Oregonian,* 77 percent of respondents wanted no expansion of the growth boundary; only 8 percent voted for a "market rules" option of expansion. Reader Rachel Johnson wrote, "Why in the world would I want to subsidize new construction of new factories to create new jobs for new people so we can have more air pollution, more traffic congestion, more sewage overflows and more school crowding? Then we'll build more roads and more prisons and more electric trains and more schools. Our parks will become trampled and crowded. Our river will become more polluted, and we'll have

In the 1990s the city of Portland grew by 35,000 people a year owing to its robust economy and reputation as a city that works. Citizens supported a statewide land use law that fights sprawl by establishing urban growth boundaries that provide for orderly development.

to drink out of it! Of course, we can have a big treatment plant to clean up the water and that will create jobs so more people can move here so we can have more housing starts and more roads and more shopping malls and more jobs and more people and so on."

Foreseeing that sequence of events a generation ago, Republican Governor Tom McCall had championed Oregon's land use law. When interviewer Charles Little asked the immensely popular governor if the program could be undone, McCall replied, "Well, you bet, it could be undone very easily. But I really couldn't see anybody getting elected who would advocate the undoing of these purposes. The electorate is enlightened in this state." If legislators opposed the land protection program, McCall said that the voters would "run them out on a rail."

Politics, unfortunately, is not what it was in 1974. In 1995, a new legislature came to power in Oregon under the influence of the largest campaign contributions ever. Republican lawmakers successfully chipped away at land-use provisions and passed six bills to cripple the legislation. None of the important ones became law, but only because Governor John Kitzhaber vetoed them, along with nearly fifty other bills, many of which sought to undercut environmental measures. "I had tremendous public support for the vetoes," Kitzhaber said.

"The people of Oregon still support the land use program," added Christine Cook, "but elected representatives this session are extremely beholden to development and resource extraction industries. This legislature is heavily lobbied by a very narrow spectrum of people." Pointing to a state bill mandating that local governments approve expansion of airports, Cook noted, "Development lobbyists want to rescind state oversight of land use plans. They push for local control, but only until local officials say no, and then they suddenly support new *state* controls that tell the local governments they have to allow development."

The Oregon legislature's reactionary approach, which Tom McCall thought was politically impossible, was repeated elsewhere in the Columbia Basin with shocking results.

White Salmon, Washington (foreground), lies across the Columbia from Hood River, Oregon. The quality of life in such communities is threatened by a movement to make it impossible for local governments to control developers.

THE REAL THREAT TO PRIVATE PROPERTY VALUES

In 1995, after being presented with an initiative petition sponsored by development groups, the Washington legislature passed the Private Property Regulatory Fairness Act, perhaps the most extreme property rights measure adopted in America. This takings law required state or local government to pay for any loss of market value resulting from government regulations. If a neighbor building a new home wanted to ignore the setback from a property line, the local government might have to pay that person to comply. To prevent development in high-hazard flood zones, wetlands, or mudslide areas that can cause damage to neighboring properties and require bailouts by taxpayers, state and local governments would have to buy out the developers. A local municipality might have to pay for people to comply with local zoning laws that had been on the books and supported by local communities for fifty years. Rather than a bill protecting private property rights, the "Fairness Act" threw property rights in the trash by making the most basic protections of property values impossible to enforce. Rather than supporting local control, the Act undercut all controls that people might have established in their communities.

Anybody who even *said* that he wanted to build something illegal, however absurd the scam, might have to be compensated by taxpayers for not being allowed to do it. Opponents dubbed the measure the "topless-bar-next-to-schools policy" of the state legislature. The margin was narrow, but this bill actually passed.

Though the elected officials voting for the bill never bothered to investigate this, the cost to local and state government of administering the new law would run from $300 million to $1 billion annually, according to the University of Washington's Institute for Public Policy and Management. Another $11 billion could be required for compensation costs in this measure passed by conservative politicians ostensibly opposed to taxes and public expenses.

Because the Act came to the legislature through an initiative process, it couldn't be vetoed. It could only be rescinded by a vote of the people, so opponents collected enough signatures to require a referendum to undo the measure in 1995. A builders association gave $1.1 million to defend the new private rights law. Likewise, Plum Creek Timber Company helped pay for the campaign, as did other logging firms with their eyes on real estate development. The State Farm Bureau, realtors, and developers all supported the assumption that maximum development is the right of each property owner, no matter what problems he creates and what cost he requires of taxpayers.

A *cause célèbre* of both the property rights movement on one side and heavily outspent environmentalists on the other, the November 1995 ballot was regarded nationwide as a bellwether; other property rights laws were being considered in many states.

The referendum to rescind the right-wing measure succeeded by a landslide 3-2 margin. Washington was the third state to vote down a takings law in statewide ballots, leading David Socolow of the American Resources Information Network to question, "If [property rights] is such a grassroots movement, why do they keep trying to get in the back door of state legislatures?"

Similar far-right movements declaring county governments as the owners of federal land ran rampant in the West in the 1990s, with residents of the stunningly beautiful Wallowa County, Oregon voting for a measure that insisted that Forest Service and Bureau of Land Management land didn't belong to the federal government. Picking up where these absurd legal claims ended, antigovernment terrorists bombed Forest Service

RIGHT: *Walla Walla, Washington, is one of many towns with outstanding amenities as a place to live and work. The leaders elected to political offices will determine whether or not communities here avoid the problems that plague other growing regions of the country.*

offices in Nevada, a conservation officer was murdered in Idaho, and various militias and "freemen" maintained that they were above the law on land use and other matters. Congressional backing of the antigovernment mania reached a zenith when Idaho Representative Helen Chenoweth supported action to ban federal law enforcement agents from carrying firearms for their self-defense in Idaho.

A QUESTION OF REPRESENTATION

As with the salmon and forests of the Columbia River Basin, the fate of the landscape will be decided by the people who voters send to office. A 1991 Gallup Poll found that Americans were as supportive of environmental quality as ever, or more so, with 71 percent saying that environmental protection should be given priority even at

risk of curbing economic growth. And over the years Northwesterners were typically more supportive of environmental protection than people in other regions. Nonetheless, national political representatives such as Linda Smith in Washington, Wes Cooley in Oregon, and Helen Chenoweth in Idaho called for state takeover of the public's federal land, an action likely to lead to privatization and development. And in local politics, the old-boy network was alive and well. "People in Hood River, Oregon are very active supporters of land protection in the Columbia River Gorge," said Lauri Aunin, "but the county commissioners don't reflect that view."

With a long-standing perspective on land use politics, geographer Ken Hammond of Central

Washington University said, "While I expect developers to do what they do, I expect county officials to stand between them and the rest of us. Well, it doesn't happen." The geographer reminded me that battles over the land can be won a thousand times but lost only once, and as long as people who will sell away the Basin's remaining heritage of open space and environmental quality get elected, the losses will continue. "The real estate lobby pays for the political campaigns," he noted, "and then the county uses public money to fight the real estate lobby's battles. Opposing them, we use our own money and pay on both sides."

Seeking solutions to long-term problems in her state, Senator Patty Murray of Washington said, "The challenge will always be looking at the short-term versus the long-term. We need to take a better approach, but to do that in the current political climate will be very difficult."

Changing the political climate is the only choice for the people of the Northwest and northern Rockies who want to see lasting qualities and real property value in their homeland. People who care about the land and the communities need to be elected.

The voters in Jackson, Wyoming sent one of those people to office. In considering a new Teton County plan, which ultimately advanced the cause of long-term values, Commissioner Steve Thomas reflected on the importance of choices and opportunities relevant in the 1990s but equally so in all the decades to come. "We currently have a unique opportunity to have an impact on the future of this valley. When we get lost in the details of this draft, we need to remember why we started this process. It was to protect our valley and way of life—the beauty and the wild things. The valley's future is in our hands. I only hope posterity will look back and be proud of what we did."

LEFT: *Mount Hood and other Cascade peaks tower over the Columbia Basin where the force of uncontrolled development is being battled by people trying to protect their environment and homeland.*

CHAPTER FIVE

THE FATE OF A RIVER BASIN

To stay the course that we've pursued for 150 years in the Columbia River Basin leads to grim consequences for people living or visiting in this special place. But hopelessness is not the theme of this story. In the fight for chinook salmon, for example, the hopeless story is the one that pretends salmon are worthless or never existed. To not know about the losses or the efforts required to reverse them is where real despair awaits, because that view accepts an emptier world. Those who would allow extinction would have us live without the assets, the blessings, the rich inheritance of the natural earth. Before long, people would never know the difference between a good life and a mediocre one. A view based on knowledge and reverence for life—not ignorance—is where hope must lie.

No matter how bad a situation gets, people can have hope as long as they have a vision of what might be. A vision for the Columbia Basin

LEFT: *The Imnaha River of northeastern Oregon flows toward Hells Canyon of the Snake River.*

would presumably include the assets that draw people here to live. But if the vision isn't clear in mind, people can easily lose what they came for; it will disappear, one piece at a time, and the losses won't be recognized until it's too late. Once people know clearly what they want, many are willing to take action. Some of today's leaders have this kind of vision for the future of the Columbia Basin.

The Columbia River Gorge east of White Salmon, Washington.

Governor John Kitzhaber of Oregon reflected, "The Columbia River is a symbol, and it will be refreshing if its salmon serve to bring the Northwest back together as a region." Touching on a vision for the future in his inaugural address, Governor Kitzhaber said, "We dwell in a rare and lovely place, where the flame of hope is not yet extinguished. More than half a century ago, a visitor here said that Oregon was as close as man could come to paradise on earth. I believe Oregon's greatness can rival its natural beauty. . . . As long as we live within these borders, and share

in the blessings and bounties of this small green corner of God's earth, we owe something in return. We owe something to each other. What we get, we must give back in equal measure. Let us begin today, one state, one people, one destiny."

Kitzhaber's vision of working together for the future and not only for profits is being pursued in many places. Joy Huber of the Rivers Council of Washington said, "If you work on your watershed, you have an opportunity to work with your neighbors in ways that have been blocked for a long time. Being active at this level is a chance to exercise civic responsibility in a context that makes sense, one where people can make a difference. People *want* to make a difference. People need to be reconnected to their places and to each other, and when they are, a new quality of government can emerge. We're trying to rebuild the idea of community, based on natural resources that we all share."

Going beyond the concepts, Huber and her council have sparked efforts on streams throughout the state. She said, "Let me be specific. We recently had a field trip to Sinking Creek, which once flowed all the time but now dries up. We expected fifteen people but sixty-five came. It was an incredible day. People who had fought over water talked to each other. As the meeting progressed, the discussion turned from legal rights—whose water is it?—to the question, 'What can we do to solve this problem?' When people looked at what needs to be done, their natural instinct was to care for each other. In looking at the stream, and imagining a vision of what it could again become, people with fifteen years of painful experience behind them were ready to figure out what steps they could take." That model of sixty-five people's experience in one afternoon—almost accidental—is being repeated across the watershed and sometimes reenacted at a grand scale.

British Columbians took giant strides toward a better vision of the future during Premier Mike Harcourt's term from 1991 to 1996. While environmental programs at similar statewide levels had stalled out in the United States, and progressive leaders such as John Kitzhaber were mainly engaged in holding the line against blatantly vested interests with no vision whatsoever except for their own bottom line, Premier Harcourt was able to forge ahead with reforms that had been ignored or opposed by administrations before him. The province sponsored a consensus process to plan for forest use. "We've seen enormous public involvement with thousands of British Columbians participating," Harcourt said. "This is in contrast to the past, when the big players—timber, mining, and B.C. Hydro—made their plans and got the government to rubber-stamp them."

The province joined a national Canadian Heritage Rivers Program, and under a new provincial rivers system, seven streams were dedicated for protection in 1996. The free-flowing upper Columbia may be considered in future listings, according to Heritage Rivers Chairman Mark Angelo. Healthy rivers are clearly a part of the vision many British Columbians hold. "Rivers and fish have become a huge issue in the past few years," Angelo said. "Our Rivers Day celebration involved 30,000 people in 1995 and was the largest event of its kind in North America. Interest in grassroots stewardship is exploding in B.C."

Regarding his vision for the future, Premier Harcourt said, "The days of shortsighted policies and short-term profits are gone, replaced with a long-term strategy for renewing our forests, reinvesting in the land, and preserving our rich environmental heritage for future generations. We're doing exciting things, but in a balanced way."

After Premier Harcourt retired, his successor in the New Democratic Party, Glen Clark, was voted in. The vote served to validate the party's progress on natural resoures, as environmental issues were heavily debated in the latter days of the campaign. Capturing a feeling of the times that will go beyond his term in office, Harcourt said, "Environmental protection and economic common sense don't have to conflict. And in the long run, they can't."

An old-time approach presumed that environmental protection countered economic development, but the inextricable ties between the two are now well established. In 1993, the economies and environmental programs of all fifty states were compared by the Institute for Southern Studies and, across the board, the states with the best environmental programs had the healthiest economies and vice versa. Oregon, for example, placed ninth in environmental protection and eighth in economic health.

Even more to the point, a landmark report issued by thirty economists in 1995 and edited by Dr. Thomas Power confirmed the connection in the Pacific Northwest. *Economic Well-Being and Environmental Protection in the Pacific Northwest* reported that the four-state region saw an 18 percent increase in jobs between 1988 and 1994 and a 24 percent increase in personal, real income. The economic growth rate was twice the national average. All this occurred in spite of declines in resource extraction jobs such as logging.

Personal income of resource extraction workers between 1969 and 1993 dropped from 7 percent of the regional total to 5 percent, and income from farming, ranching, and agricultural services dropped from 11 to 6 percent. The economists found that "the Pacific Northwest does not have to choose between jobs and the environment. Quite the opposite: a healthy environment is a major stimulus for a healthy economy." The report maintained that a principal reason for the region's economic health is its quality of life. "The region is perceived as promising a superior, attractive environment in which to live, work, and do business. . . . Because people care where they live and because businesses care where people choose to live, environmental quality has a positive impact on the local economy."

Regarding efforts to prop up the extractive industries with subsidies and environmental exemptions—both being pushed by the region's congressional delegation in 1996—the economists warned, "Environmental degradation has impoverished other regions; it can impoverish this one too. . . . Political forces, even powerful special interests, cannot bring back the economy of a past era. The unique natural resources of the Pacific Northwest remain among its most important economic assets. But the new jobs and income that are vital to the region's economic future will depend more on the *protection* of those assets than on their degradation."

Aware of the trends and striving to put this necessary merger of economic and environmental concerns into a workable relationship, Senator Patty Murray of Washington said that her vision of the Columbia is "a river that's cared for, that will offer a commercial and sport fishery, that will pro-

vide for a place to live, to work, to rest, and to relax. The balance is something we have to focus on." Recognizing that it's possible to have a working river *and* a living river, she added, "We can't avoid the fact that our economy is tied to the river, but we can't ignore that the river must be healthy. The worst legacy we could leave would be to prevent our grandchildren from living with the qualities we now have in the Columbia River Basin."

While agreeing in concept that protection of the economy and environment are both needed, Governor Phil Batt of Idaho said in 1996 that he did not see great changes or new outlooks in the political winds. "Idaho is a conservative state. We will prevail in protecting jobs and free enterprise."

A receptivity to change, however, can be seen through much of the Columbia River Basin, from the new policies of British Columbia's provincial government to the land use plan for Teton County, Wyoming. "The attitudes *are* changing," said Angus Duncan, former chairman of the Northwest Power Planning Council. "We're not succeeding in fixing things immediately, but people are looking more at the whole picture. Throughout history, the river basin's been separated over and over, chopped up into fragments. We need to reassemble them so that the system works for creatures like the salmon. The whole watershed has to be the planning unit. Otherwise, the human impulse is to focus on the foreground and leave the future to take care of itself. The issue of our time is in changing people's attitudes about the Basin, and valuing the whole rather than valuing the parts separately."

When the pieces are separated, they are more easily commodified. Parts can be sold without

realizing what else is being ruined. The men who logged the Santiam basin probably didn't think about their work aggravating floods in the Willamette Valley, or about the economic loss and human suffering that resulted from those floods. The people working in the aluminum plants probably don't think much about fishermen and cannery workers who lost their jobs when the salmon populations crashed.

In this larger scale of concern that Duncan advocated, it's evident that few people think of the Columbia as one basin. People in the Willamette Valley may regard *it* as a basin, but only peripherally attached to the Columbia. The Yakima watershed is often thought of in halves—the Kittitas and Yakima Valleys, but the Yakima River Watershed Council is tearing that boundary down. Idahoans think of themselves as Snake River dependent, but their thoughts seldom extend downstream, or for that matter, upstream to Wyoming, where most of southern Idaho's water comes from. Ironically, the Bonneville Power Administration has the most Basinwide outlook. It certainly regards the waters as being connected, though the linkages it sees do

Sunset at McDonald Lake in Glacier National Park, Montana

Moonrise over Sawtooth Peak in Idaho.

systems around freeways and fiber-optic cables rather than around the path of water. Has anyone looked at the river as a whole? The tribes probably come the closest."

Recognizing that great changes are necessary, Ted Strong of the Columbia River Inter-Tribal Fish Commission said, "These rivers are the heartbeat of the earth. We have no other laws before the laws of nature. All others are secondary. The Columbia River Basin has to be looked upon and planned for as one system. That's the tribal view. Watershed sustainability has to be as important to us as democracy."

Senator Patty Murray shared that sense of wholeness. "In Washington, we inherit what happens upriver. We contribute to what flows into the ocean. Though local control sounds nice, all these states and British Columbia are tied together with one future."

Many opportunities await once this all-pervasive interconnectedness is recognized, apparent in the debates around salmon, forests, and open space. One of many imaginative examples can be seen with the group River Network, a national organization based in Portland. It has launched a Willamette River effort aimed at restoring some of the natural flood-control capacities of the river. "The Willamette has been so channelized that it doesn't do the free work of flood control it once did," said Phil Wallin, founder of the group. "The water comes down faster because the spongelike wetlands and the braided river channels, with a six-mile-wide, forested floodway, are gone." Hydrologists for River Network reported that better management of 20,000 to 50,000 acres of floodplain wetlands could reduce peak floods by 18 percent in some

not form an organic whole but rather an energy grid with square corners, breaker boxes, and surge protectors. Andy Kerr of the Oregon Natural Resources Council said, "We're building our social areas. Wallin said, "We hope to buy land and easements to restore some of that capability, and we'll be getting a healthier river in the bargain."

Just as wetlands, floodplains, and flood flows are linked together, so are the rest of the elements of the Columbia, and the entire Basin is tied to the rest of the continent and world. Washington growers now sell apples to Japan. What will that mean for irrigation, diversions from the river, hydropower, and salmon? Timber shipped overseas certainly affects the forests, watersheds, and mill-workers of the Northwest.

Population growth illustrates the ultimate linkage to other places. The influx of people to Portland, Yakima, and Jackson is directly related to the population growth of the United States and even Mexico. People spill out from areas of high population, such as Seattle and San Francisco, to low density areas, such as Idaho and Montana. People migrate from areas of poor opportunity, such as North Dakota and Mexico, to havens of good opportunity, such as Corvallis and Boise. They are drawn from areas of degraded quality, such as Los Angeles and Houston, to places where the water is clean, the crime rate low, and the natural world close enough to reach out and touch. Those trends have people moving into the Columbia Basin, and all those factors tie the fate of the Northwest and northern Rockies to that of people and politics elsewhere.

During the next twenty years, the population of the United States is projected to increase by nearly 21 percent. The birthrate of most of the U.S. is quite low; more than half of all growth is now a result of immigration from other countries and from the high birthrates of new immigrants. With immigration at 1996 levels, the population of the country will grow by another 160 million in only sixty years, and a high rate of growth will continue indefinitely (the 1996 population was 265 million). If immigration were reduced from the current estimate of 1 million people a year to 100,000, the nation's population would stabilize at about 300 million in the next century, according to analysts cited by the group Negative Population Growth. A Roper poll found that 54 percent of Americans supported an immigration reduction to less than 100,000, and 70 percent supported a level of 300,000 or lower—less than one-third the current rate.

As the national population increases, some regions of the country will scarcely grow at all because people from those places will be going to the Northwest, northern Rockies, and other choice spots of desirability, which will consequently grow much faster than the average. More people will mean more development, increased electricity use, crowded recreation sites, higher real estate prices, crime, congestion, and an impoverished environment in which to raise children. Angus Duncan said, "The really big issue is whether or not we are willing to contain our population. Population pressure affects everything. And population growth multiplied by technological change has been devastating to the Columbia."

The best plans to manage growth, which is all that even progressive programs seek, will ultimately fail if there isn't eventually an end to growth. Even if the urbanization of forestland is reduced from the current 75,000 acres per year to half that amount, or even a tenth, many of the finest low-elevation forestlands will eventually be consumed—it's merely a matter of how far ahead one is willing to look. Though the population issue is virtually ignored by governments at every level, reductions in the rate of growth are possible through reduced immigration. It's up to the people elected to Congress. Increased family planning, campaigns against teen pregnancy, education on the benefits of small families, and reduction of economic incentives such as tax breaks for large families might all encourage slower growth and ultimately a sustainable population level. International policies that encourage family planning and stable economies can perhaps reduce some of the pressure to immigrate. Without stabilization of population in the United States and in the region, virtually every effort to keep the Columbia Basin a desirable place will ultimately be doomed as resource demands and crowding affect all aspects of life—as Portland becomes like gridlocked San Francisco, as Boise becomes like urban-stressed Portland, as Coeur d'Alene becomes like smoggy Boise, as Invermere becomes like bustling Coeur d'Alene.

While population growth increases, each day will see choices being made about the Columbia Basin, and many of the important decisions will be made by elected representatives. Will their actions reflect the long-term good that Senator Patty Murray spoke of, or will they reflect the short-term interests that wield so much influence over everything from old-growth forests to urban growth boundaries? Tim Stearns of Save Our Wild Salmon said, "Politicians won't lead until you create a constituency for them. In the Northwest, we need to make it safe to be a leader again."

The environment, long ignored and given short shrift in political campaigns, is an issue whose time has come in the Columbia Basin. Why shouldn't elections be driven by environ-

mental awareness? Among Idaho's population of 1.2 million people, more than 300,000 own a fishing or hunting license; people with outdoor interests are a major political constituency. In Oregon, voters are among the most attuned in the nation to environmental issues, proven by repeated support for the nation's best land use planning law. In Washington, a population boom for years has owed its existence to people seeking quality of life. Montana prides itself as the "last best place." So why do these people send politicians to office who favor aluminum subsidies over salmon, who vote for salvage logging to cut ancient forests that are alive and well, who vote for laws that seek to cripple state and local land use planning? Many of the debates and slogans that elections hinge upon have nothing to do with questions of how the Columbia Basin will be used and protected, though these issues of health, jobs, and children are among the most central to people's lives.

Thirty-four percent of the Idaho state legislature in 1996 listed themselves as ranchers, farmers, or agribusinessmen in a state where only 5 percent of the people were engaged in those professions. The state's congressional delegation racked up an environmental voting record of zero in 1995—distinguishing Idaho by scoring the only zero in the nation. The Washington legislature in 1995 voted for a takings law that was overturned 3-2 by the voters. Why aren't those elected officials representing the people? The revealing clue lies in Oregon, where extractive industries contributed $2 million to state legislature candidates in 1994 while environmental organizations contributed $46,000. The resulting legislature passed dozens of bills to gut environmental laws. In Washington, where salmon enjoy widespread recognition as a symbol of the region, Senator Patty Murray said, "I find myself the lonely defender of the salmon. The people in politics today seem to care a lot about power but not much about the fish. The people who vote will go to battle for the good things in life, but by the time they do, it's often too late."

The alternatives are very clear, as they have been throughout recent history and as they will likely remain. In many elections, future-thinking candidates run for office, giving voters a meaningful choice. In the 1996 U.S. Senate race in Idaho, Walt Minnick unsuccessfully challenged Larry Craig. Minnick said, "It's almost universal in the Rocky Mountains that political leaders favor consumptive uses over quality of life considerations. Many of the people in power still view the modern West as a frontier to be conquered instead of a place for your children to live. But the population and the economy of the West have changed. We need to select political leaders at all levels who view the region through the prism of the twenty-first century rather than the

nineteenth. As more people see the quality of life disappearing, they'll get angry, and when they reach a critical mass, change will occur. I think it's happening now."

The fate of the Columbia Basin, with all its water and land, depends on people becoming involved in the future. Without support for political candidates who work toward a positive vision of the future, the entire watershed will default to the people who seek only personal gain and short-term profit.

From his home near the southeastern end of the Columbia's watershed, Shoshone and Bannock elder Lionel Boyer said, "As Indians, our survival depends on our linkage with the past." In this, he recognized that honoring the earth and the ancestors requires care of our homeland for the future. Watersheds need to be repaired, and the best of what remains needs to be saved for generations to come. "Now is the time for all of us to work toward these objectives. Much has been lost, but now it's up to you, and those you talk with, to turn this around."

Acknowledgments

Ann Vileisis, my wife, participated in many ways in the creation of this book: she offered insights from her perspective as a writer, historian, and educator; she enjoyed exploring new reaches of the Columbia Basin with me; she edited the manuscript with great skill and provided honest reactions to my work.

I would not have written the book if it weren't for the confidence of Jon Beckmann, who tracked me down in the spring of 1995 on the Green River of Utah to ask if I'd be willing to work on a book about the modern day Columbia Basin. His attention as editor of the book was always welcome and helpful. Likewise, the project began as an idea of the editors and board of The Mountaineers, and I'd like to thank former press director Donna DeShazo and her group of professionals for their excellent work.

Scores of people contributed information and interviews for *The Columbia;* many of their names appear in the text. The time and knowledge of all are appreciated. For special insight, ideas, and leads to interesting themes, I enjoyed the help of Mason Williams, Angus Duncan, Mark Angelo, Charles Ray, Tim Stearns, and Pat Ford. Chapters or portions of chapters were reviewed by Dick Anderwald, Mark Angelo, Bob Doppelt, Angus Duncan, Ken Hammond, John Harrison, John Horgan, Clarence Moriwaki, Debbie Randall, Charles Ray, Merritt Tuttle, and Morris Uebelacker. The staff of the Northwest Power Planning Council were exceptionally helpful in providing information and tracking down difficult-to-verify data.

I benefited from the work of a number of writers, especially Kathie Durbin and Paul Koberstein, formerly of the *Oregonian* and now of *Cascadia Times,* a monthly newspaper that performs a great service for Northwesterners by informing them about environmental news of the region. Fine books by Joseph Cone, William Dietrich, Timothy Egan, Blaine Harden, Nancy Langston, Anthony Netboy, Elliott Norse, Keith Petersen, David Seideman, and others were useful, and would likely be interesting to anyone further pursuing the literature of the Basin.

My special thanks go to Margot and Alan Hunt of Kelly, Wyoming, and to Kaz Thea of Portland for the use of their comfortable homes while they were working or traveling elsewhere.

LEFT: *Sunrise at Grand Teton National Park, Wyoming.*

Sources

Mileages are based on Army Corps of Engineers calculations in the United States. For Canada, I scaled mileage from the 1:200,000 scale map of Banff, Kootenay, and Yoho National Parks by Parks Canada, 1985, and from the 1:600,000 scale map of South Eastern British Columbia by Surveys and Resource Mapping Branch, Ministry of Environment, Lands, and Parks, Victoria, B.C., 1992.

INTRODUCTION:
A PLACE OF GREAT CONSEQUENCE

See sources of more detailed information in the following chapters.

CHAPTER 1:
ONE WATERSHED

Amaral, Grant. *Idaho: The Whitewater State.* Garden Valley, Idaho: Watershed Books, 1990. Descriptions of Idaho rivers.

Blakeless, John. *The Journals of Lewis and Clark.* New York: Mentor Books, 1964.

Cody, Robin. *Voyage of a Summer Sun: Canoeing the Columbia River.* New York: Knopf, 1995. A personal narrative of a canoe trip on the Columbia's reservoirs and remaining sections of river.

Dietrich, William. *Northwest Passage: The Great Columbia River.* New York: Simon and Schuster, 1995. Excellent popular history and modern perspective on the river.

Egan, Timothy. *The Good Rain.* New York: Vintage Departures, 1991. Includes fascinating reporting on the Columbia Basin.

Fisher, Hank. *The Floater's Guide to Montana.* Helena, Mont.: Falcon Press, 1986.

Foreman, David, and Howie Wolke. *The Big Outside: A Descriptive Inventory of the Big Wilderness Areas of the U.S.* Tuscon, Ariz.: Ned Ludd Books, 1989. Description of wild areas of the Basin.

Frost, Evan. "A Preliminary Conservation Plan for the Columbia Mountains." *Wild Earth,* Summer 1995. Natural history of the Columbia Mountains in B.C.

Gadd, Ben. *Handbook of the Canadian Rockies.* Jasper, Alberta: Corax Press, 1986. An excellent compendium of the Canadian Rockies.

Harden, Blaine. *A River Lost: The Life and Death of the Columbia.* New York: W. W. Norton, 1996. An engrossing portrait of the river as seen through this fine journalist's eyes and through those of the people he interviews. Includes a revealing chapter on Hanford.

Hume, Mark. *The Run of the River: Portraits of Eleven British Columbia Rivers.* Vancouver, B.C.: New Star Books, 1992. This excellent book includes a chapter on the Columbia.

Kiyomura, Cathy. "Saving the Slough." *Oregonian,* Nov. 23, 1995. The Columbia Slough in Portland.

Mathews, Daniel. *Cascade-Olympic Natural History.* Portland:

Audubon Society of Portland, 1990. An informative natural history guide.

McNulty, Tim, with photographs by Pat O'Hara. *Washington's Wild Rivers: The Unfinished Work.* Seattle: The Mountaineers, 1990. A book of beautiful photographs and profiles of Washington rivers, including Columbia tributaries.

North, Douglass A. *Washington Whitewater, Vol. 1.* Seattle: The Mountaineers, 1988.

———. *Washington Whitewater, Vol. 2.* Seattle: The Mountaineers, 1987.

Northwest Environmental Advocates. *Columbia River—Troubled Waters.* Brochure and map. Portland, 1992. Water quality and other information.

Olsen, Ken. "At Hanford, the real estate is hot." *High Country News.* Jan. 22, 1996. Future of the Hanford Reservation.

Oregon State Parks and Oregon State Marine Board. *Willamette River Recreation: Guide.* Salem, Ore.: 1995.

Oregonian. "House-Senate panel approves boost in nuclear waste cleanup." Oct. 26, 1995.

———. "County officials will ask judge to spare Hanford test reactor." Nov. 6, 1995.

———. "U.S. report criticizes management of defunct Hanford plutonium plant." Nov. 25, 1995. These newspaper articles cover modern problems with Hanford waste and Tri-Cities support for the nuclear industry.

Peirce, Neal R., and Jerry Hagstrom. *The Book of America.* New York: W. W. Norton, 1983. Excellent profiles of the states.

Pratt-Johnson, Betty. *Whitewater Trips and Hot Springs in the Kootenays of British Columbia.* Vancouver, B.C.: Adventure Publishing, 1989.

U.S. Forest Service. *Upper Klickitat River Wild and Scenic River Study Report.* Portland, 1990.

———. *Upper White Salmon River Wild and Scenic River Study Report.* Portland, 1990.

White, Richard. *The Organic Machine.* New York: Hill and Wang, 1995. A short history of the Basin.

Willamette Kayak and Canoe Club. *Soggy Sneakers: Guide to Oregon Rivers.* Corvallis, Ore.: The Club, 1986.

Williams, Chuck. *Bridge of the Gods, Mountains of Fire: A Return to the Columbia Gorge.* Friends of the Earth: Washington, D.C., 1980. A book of interesting photos and text on the Columbia Gorge.

Interviews

Nina Bell, Northwest Environmental Advocates, Portland

Julia Cundliffe, realtor, Golden, B.C.

Kevin Finnegan, bookstore owner, Golden, B.C.

Richard Fish, Cominco, Trail, B.C.

Don Francis, Sierra Club, Portland

John Horgan, Office of the Premier, Victoria, B.C.

Wayne Houlbrook, tour guide, Golden, B.C.

Brent Humphrey, Office of the Premier, Victoria, B.C.

Graham Kenyon, Cominco, Trail, B.C.

Dennis Todd, biologist and river traveler, Eugene, Ore.

CHAPTER 2:
THE LONG SWIM HOME

Berg, Laura. "Tribes Release Salmon Restoration Plan." *Wana Chinook Tymoo,* magazine of the Columbia River Inter-Tribal Fish Commission, Issues 2 and 3, 1995. Discusses the tribes' plan for salmon recovery.

Bogaard, Joseph. "Giving Voice to Salmon." *Illahee,* published by the Institute for Environmental Studies, University of Washington, Winter 1994. This entire issue covers many aspects of the salmon crisis.

Bullard, Oral. *Crisis on the Columbia,* Portland: Touchstone, 1968. Historical perspective on the salmon problem.

Columbia Basin Institute. *The Role of Irrigation Subsidy in the Bonneville Power Administration's Death Spiral.* Portland, 1995. Economic information and data on irrigation subsidies in the Basin.

Cone, Joseph. *A Common Fate: Endangered Salmon and the People of the Pacific Northwest.* New York: Henry Holt, 1995. An account of the modern salmon problem, emphasizing the people who are involved and covering coastal streams.

Cone, Joseph, and Sandy Ridlington, eds. *The Northwest Salmon Crisis: A Documentary History.* Corvallis: Oregon State University Press, 1996.

Connelly Joel. "Public wants to aid salmon, poll reveals." *Seattle Post-Intelligencer,* March 28, 1995. Public opinion about salmon and costs of recovery.

Ford, Pat, ed. "Northwest Salmon at the Crossroads." *High Country News,* April 22, 1991, entire issue. Excellent coverage of the issue as of 1991.

Friends of the Earth, Taxpayers for Common Sense, and the Save Our Wild Salmon Coalition. *River of Red Ink.* Seattle: Friends of the Earth, 1996. An exposé of Columbia River Basin subsidies.

Idaho Office of the Governor. *Snake River Salmon: National Treasure at Risk of Extinction.* Boise, 1993. Idaho's case for drawdown of lower Snake River reservoirs during the Andrus administration.

Idaho Rivers United. *They Shoulda Missed the Boat.* Boise: Idaho Rivers United, 1995, pamphlet. Information on the problems of barging salmon and steelhead.

Independent Scientific Group for the Northwest Power Planning Council. *Return to the River.* Richard N. Williams, Chair. Portland, 1996.

Institute for Fisheries Resources. *The Cost of Doing Nothing: The Economic Burden of Salmon Declines in the Columbia River Basin.* Eugene, Ore., 1996.

Koberstein, Paul. "Fishy Science." *Cascadia Times,* January 1996. Reports on the scientific panels advising salmon recovery agencies.

Lansing, Philip S. *An Economic Analysis of Four Federal Dams on the Lower Snake River.* Boise: Idaho Rivers United, 1995, pamphlet. Data on the costs of the dams and the proposal to eliminate them.

Maxwell, Jessica. "Swimming with Salmon." *Natural History,* Sept. 1995. Focus on ocean conditions.

Meehan, Brian T., and Joan Laatz Jewett. "River of Ghosts." *Oregonian,* special report, Oct. 29, 1995. An extensive report on the salmon in 1995.

Meggs, Geoff. *Salmon: The Decline of the B.C. Fishery.* Vancouver, B.C.: Douglas and McIntyre, 1991. Excellent book about salmon in British Columbia.

National Marine Fisheries Service. *Proposed Snake River Salmon Recovery Plan.* Seattle, March 1995. The official plan under the Endangered Species Act.

National Research Council. *Upstream: Salmon and Society in the Pacific Northwest.* Washington, D. C., Nov. 1995. The controversial report of this scientific panel.

Nehlsen, Willa. "Salmon Stocks at Risk: Beyond 214." *Conservation Biology,* Sept. 1995. A follow-up on Nehlsen's landmark article about the status of endangered salmon.

Netboy, Anthony. *Salmon of the Pacific Northwest.* Portland: Binfords and Mort, 1958. An interesting book for its time.

———. *The Columbia River Salmon and Steelhead Trout.* Seattle: University of Washington Press, 1980. An excellent report as of 1980.

———. *The Salmon: Their Struggle for Survival.* Boston: Houghton and Mifflin, 1974. This is a landmark of environmental history in the Northwest, a must for anyone seeking a thorough knowledge of salmon worldwide.

Northwesterners for More Fish. *Northwesterners for More Fish: A Program of Project Common Sense.* A memo to "Invited Guests to Salmon Recovery Meeting in Spokane." Jan. 31, 1996. Available at Idaho Rivers United, Boise.

Northwest Power Planning Council. *Northwest Energy News.* Issues from 1989 through 1996. Fine sources for latest-breaking news and policy.

Oregon Natural Resources Council. "Canned Salmon: How the Aluminum Industry Kills Fish." *Wild Oregon.* Newsletter of the Council, April 1994. An exposé on subsidies and the aluminum industry.

Pacific Rivers Council. *Restoration: A Blueprint for Saving Wild Fish and Watersheds in the Northwest.* Eugene: the Council, 1994.

Palmer, Tim. *The Snake River: Window to the West.* Washington, D.C.: Island Press, 1991. Thorough coverage of the Snake River.

———.*Lifelines: The Case for River Conservation.* Washington, D. C.: Island Press, 1994. This book begins with a nationwide perspective on the salmon.

Save Our Wild Salmon Coalition. *Wild Salmon Forever.* Seattle, 1994. A compendium of information and conservationists' proposals.

U.S. House Committee on Natural Resources, BPA Task Force. *BPA at a Crossroads.* Washington, D. C., 1994.

Volkman, John M. *A Meeting of Opposites—Is Sustainable Use of the Columbia River Possible?* Portland, Ore.: Northwest Power Planning Council, 1995, unpublished paper. A thoughtful reflection on the salmon crisis.

Walth, Brent. "BPA deal's waiver of fish law risks veto." *Oregonian,* Oct. 20, 1995. News about the price cap of 1995 and threat to the Endangered Species Act.

Walth, Brent. "The Northwest's clout will go with Hatfield." *Oregonian,* Dec. 3, 1995. A revealing profile of Senator Hatfield's power and influence, including the incident with Energy Secretary Hazel O'Leary.

Watkins, T. H. "What's Wrong With The Endangered Species Act?" *Audubon,* Jan. 1996. A report on the Act's threatened status in 1996.

Interviews

Cecil Andrus, former Governor of Idaho, Boise

Rocky Barker, journalist, *Idaho Statesman*

Phil Batt, Governor of Idaho

Ed Chaney, biologist, Eagle, Idaho

Angus Duncan, former Chairman, Northwest Power Planning Council

Dawn Edwards, Army Corps of Engineers, Walla Walla, Wash.

Pat Ford, Save Our Wild Salmon, Boise

Perry Grubber, Bonneville Power Administration

Randall Hardy, Chief Administrator, Bonneville Power Administration

John Harrison, Northwest Power Planning Council

Barry Hurst, Bonneville Power Administration

Jim Lazar, economics consultant, Olympia, Wash.

Bruce Lovelin, Columbia River Alliance for Fish, Commerce, and Communities

Walt Minnick, U.S. Senate candidate, Boise

Patty Murray, U.S. Senate, Seattle

Peter Paquet, Northwest Power Planning Council

Keith Petersen, author, Pullman, Wash.

Charles Ray, Idaho Rivers United, McCall, Idaho

Will Reed, Idaho Department of Fish and Game, Boise

Jack Robertson, Deputy Administrator, Bonneville Power Administration

Ed Sheets, Executive Director, Northwest Power Planning Council

Tim Stearns, Save Our Wild Salmon Coalition

Ted Strong, Executive Director, Columbia River Inter-Tribal Fish Commission

Merritt Tuttle, retired from the National Marine Fisheries Service, Portland

John Volkman, Northwest Power Planning Council

Wendy Wilson, Idaho Rivers United, Boise

CHAPTER 3:
THE FOREST

Anderson, Molly Dee. "The Forest or the Trees." *Seattle,* Sept. 1995. An article on the Northwest Forest Plan and salvage logging issues.

British Columbia Ministry of Forests. *British Columbia's Forest Renewal Plan.* Victoria, 1994.

———. *Forest Practices Code: Summary of Presentations by Stakeholder Groups.* Victoria, 1994. Critiques of the province's plan.

Cascadia Times. "Northwest Now Has More Roads than Rivers." Jan. 1996. A report on mileage and effects of forest roads.

Dietrich, William. *The Final Forest.* New York: Penguin, 1992. A fine book on the old-growth debate, focusing on people and centered on the Olympic Peninsula of Washington.

Durbin, Kathie, and Paul Koberstein. "Forests in Distress." *Oregonian,* a special report, Oct. 15, 1995. Superb coverage of politics of the 1980s, overview of old-growth issues, and the political pressure to log.

Durbin, Kathie. *Tree Huggers: Victory, Defeat, and Renewal in the Northwest Ancient Forest Campaign.* Seattle: The Mountaineers, 1996. Indispensable, thorough coverage of the old-growth debate.

Ervin, Keith. *Fragile Majesty.* Seattle: The Mountaineers, 1989. A fine book about the old-growth issue as of 1989.

Karr, James R. and Ellen W. Chu, eds. *Interim Protection for Late-Successional Forests, Fisheries, and Watersheds: National Forests East of the Cascade Crest, Oregon and Washington.* Bethesda, Md.: Eastside Forests Scientific Society Panel, The Wildlife Society, 1994. An extraordinary catalog of information, data, and recommendations about forests and streams of eastern Oregon and Washington.

Koberstein, Paul, and Kathie Durbin. "Federal Agencies Square Off in Idaho." *Cascadia Times,* Feb. 1996. The controversy over salvage logging and the Thunderbolt sale.

Langston, Nancy. *Forest Dreams, Forest Nightmares.* Seattle: University of Washington Press, 1995. A revealing history of forestry in the Blue Mountains.

Mazza, Patrick. "An Act of God?" *Cascadia Times,* March 1995. Reports on runoff studies by Gordon Grant of the Forest Service's Pacific Northwest Forest and Range Experiment Station and Julia Jones of Oregon State University; also on runoff studies by Dennis Harr, University of Washington.

Norse, Elliott. *Ancient Forests of the Pacific Northwest.* Washington, D.C.: Island Press, 1990. This excellent book details the characteristics of and values to old-growth forests and the threats to them. A fine field guide, readable account of the controversy, and reference book.

Olsen, Ken. "Logged Wildlands collapse into Idaho's creeks." *High Country News,* Jan. 22, 1996. Reports on the stormwater erosion of logged lands in 1996.

Oregon Office of the Governor. *Forest Health and Timber Harvest on National Forests in the Blue Mountains of Oregon: A Report to Governor Kitzhaber.* Salem, 1995.

Pacific Rivers Council. *A Call for a Comprehensive Watershed and Wild Fish Conservation Program in Eastern Oregon and Washington.* Eugene, Ore., 1995.

———. *Freeflow.* Newsletters of the Council, 1991–95.

———. *Northern Rockies Forests and Endangered Native Fish.* Feb. 1995.

———. *Salmon Habitat in Idaho.* 1995.

———. *Wildfire and Salvage Logging.* Unpublished paper by scientists for the Council, March 1995. All of these Pacific Rivers Council documents report on the findings of scientists; they present a wealth of data and recommend solutions.

Partridge, Dr. Arthur. "Partridge Exposes 'Salvage' Hoax." *Save America's Forests,* Winter 1995–96. Dr. Partridge's testimony on salvage logging.

Save America's Forests. Entire issue on salvage logging, Winter 1995–1996. A compendium of information and the conservationists' response to the salvage rider.

Sedler, Liz. "Phantom Forests on the Kootenai." *Wild Forest Review,* Feb. 1994. Reports on the inflated estimates of old growth.

Seideman, David. "Out of the Woods." *Audubon,* July/August 1996. Reports on the new economy of the Northwest.

Shabecoff, Philip. "Greens vs. Congress: a Play-by-Play." *The Amicus Journal,* Fall 1996.

St. Clair, Jeffrey, ed. *Wild Forest Review.* Issues from 1993–96. These interesting magazines probe the politics of the old-growth debate and present the environmental case with a strong protection point of view.

U.S. Department of Agriculture, Forest Service, Pacific Northwest Forest and Range Experiment Station. *Production, Prices, Employment, and Trade in Northwest Forest Industries, Fourth Quarter 1994.* Portland, 1995. A book of data on logging and forest products.

U.S. Forest Service and Bureau of Land Management. *Upper Columbia River Basin Environmental Impact Statement Draft.* Portland: Pacific Northwest Forest and Range Experiment Station, 1996. The "Eastside" study, intended to avert endangered species gridlock.

U.S. Office of the President. *The President's Forest Plan.* Washington, D.C., 1995. A brochure summarizing the Northwest Forest Plan.

Yaffee, Steven Lewis. *The Wisdom of the Spotted Owl: Policy Lessons for a New Century.* Washington, D.C.: Island Press, 1994. This fine book includes a thorough history of the owl controversy and its policy implications.

Interviews

Bob Beckman, Columbia River Bioregional Campaign, Walla Walla, Wash.

Kent Connaughton, U.S. Forest Service, Portland

Bob Doppelt, Pacific Rivers Council, Eugene, Ore.

Mike Harcourt, Premier of British Columbia

Richard Haynes, Pacific Northwest Forest and Range Experiment Station, Portland

Rex Holloway, Forest Service, Interior Columbia Project, Walla Walla, Wash.

Andy Kerr, Oregon Natural Resources Council, Portland

John Kitzhaber, Governor of Oregon

Walt Minnick, U.S. Senate candidate, Boise

Clarence Moriwaki, U.S. Forest Service, Office of Forestry and Economic Development

Patty Murray, U.S. Senate, Seattle

Dale Robertson, former Chief, U.S. Forest Service

Jeffrey St. Clair, editor, *Wild Forest Review,* Portland

CHAPTER 4:
THE VALUE OF LAND

Bowen, Blair, Jr. "The Columbia River Gorge National Scenic Area: The Act, Its Genesis and Legislative History." *Environmental Law,* vol. 17:863, Northwestern School of Law of Lewis and Clark College, 1987. A thorough history of Gorge protection efforts.

Chilson, Peter. "Sagebrush rebels in the apple orchards." *High Country News,* June 10, 1996. Reports on Chelan County and the Washington State Growth Management Act.

Columbia River Gorge Commission. *An Overview: Columbia River Gorge National Scenic Area Management Plan.* White Salmon, Wash.: the Commission, 1994.

Jackson Hole Alliance for Responsible Planning. *Jackson Creating a Community in Balance: An Overview of the County Land Use Plan.* Jackson, Wyo.: the Alliance, 1995. Includes the quote by Steve Thomas.

Johnson, J., and R. Rasker. "Local Government: Local Business Climate and Quality of Life." *Montana Policy Review,* Fall 1993. An economic case for environmental quality protection.

Liberty, Robert. "A Choice of Futures." *Landmark,* the newsletter of 1000 Friends of Oregon, Portland, Jan. 1995. A retrospective on land use management under Oregon's state law.

Little, Charles. *The New Oregon Trail: An account of the development and passage of state land-use legislation in Oregon.* Washington, D.C.: The Conservation Foundation, 1974. Includes the interview with Tom McCall.

Mayer, James, and Steve Suo. "To readers, growth isn't a game." *Oregonian,* Nov. 15, 1995. The *Oregonian's* survey of attitudes about growth.

Nokes, R. Gregory, and Gail Kinsey Hill. "The faster the growth, the faster the tab mounts." *Oregonian,* Oct. 24, 1995. Coverage of the costs of growth.

Portland State University, Center for Population Research and Census, School of Urban and Public Affairs. *Population Estimates for Oregon: July 1, 1994.* Portland: the Center, 1994. Population estimates for Oregon. Estimates from the Northwest Power Planning Council were also used in this chapter.

River Network. *An Evaluation of Flood Management Benefits through Floodplain Restoration on the Willamette River, Oregon.* Prepared by Philip Williams and Associates. Portland: River Network, 1996. Data underpinning River Network's Willamette restoration project.

Washington State Office of Financial Management. *1995 Population Trends for Washington State.* Olympia, 1995.

Yakima County. *Vision 2010: Planning for Yakima County's Next*

Twenty Years. Yakima, 1992. Local views about planning and community.

Interviews

John Alwin, author, geographer, Central Washington University, Ellensburg, Wash.

Steve Anderson, The Nature Conservancy, Portland

Dick Anderwald, Yakima County Planner

Mark Angelo, Outdoor Recreation Council of British Columbia, Vancouver

Lauri Aunin, Friends of the Columbia River Gorge, Portland

Christine Cook, 1000 Friends of Oregon, Portland

Julia Cundliffe, realtor, Golden, B.C.

Clayton Denman, anthropologist, Central Washington University, Ellensburg, Wash.

Sue Doroff, River Network, Portland

Don Francis, Sierra Club, Portland

Scott Garland, Jackson Hole Alliance for Responsible Planning, Jackson, Wyo.

Kit Gillem, The Nature Conservancy, Portland

Ken Hammond, geographer, Central Washington University, Ellensburg, Wash.

Mike Harcourt, Premier of British Columbia

Mel Jackson, teacher and naturalist, Eugene, Ore.

Pam Leightman, Jackson Hole Alliance for Responsible Planning, Jackson, Wyo.

Debbie Randall, county planner, Kittitas County, Ellensburg, Wash.

Phil Shelton, Yakima River Watershed Council, Yakima, Wash.

Morris Uebelacker, geographer, Central Washington University, Ellensburg, Wash.

Mel Wagner, Yakima River Watershed Council, Yakima, Wash.

CHAPTER 5:
THE FATE OF A RIVER BASIN

Power, T. M., ed. *Economic Well-Being and Environmental Protection in the Pacific Northwest: A Consensus Report by Pacific Northwest Economists.* Available from T. M. Power, Economics Department, University of Montana, Missoula, Dec. 1995. An important report on the tie between economic and environmental health.

Interviews

Cecil Andrus, former Governor of Idaho, Boise

Mark Angelo, Chairman, British Columbia Heritage Rivers Board, Vancouver

Phil Batt, Governor of Idaho

Ron Beitelsbacher, former state legislator, Grangeville, Idaho

Lionel Boyer, Shoshone and Bannock Tribes, Fort Hall, Idaho

Pat Ford, Save Our Wild Salmon, Boise

Mike Harcourt, Premier of British Columbia

Joy Huber, Rivers Council of Washington, Seattle

Andy Kerr, Oregon Natural Resources Council, Portland

John Kitzhaber, Governor of Oregon

Chris Maser, ecologist and author, Corvallis, Ore.

Walt Minnick, U.S. Senate candidate, Boise

Ed Sheets, Executive Director, Northwest Power Planning Council

Tim Stearns, Save Our Wild Salmon, Seattle

Ted Strong, Executive Director, Columbia River Inter-Tribal Fish Commission, Portland

Phil Wallin, River Network, Portland

Wendy Wilson, Idaho Rivers United, Boise

Index

About the Author

Tim Palmer first encountered the Columbia while working for the U.S. Forest Service in 1969. Since then he has traveled throughout the Columbia Basin by van, canoe, and whitewater raft as well as on skis and on foot. The author of twelve books, including *The Snake River: Window to the West; America by Rivers; Lifelines: The Case for River Conservation; The Wild and Scenic Rivers of America;* and *Endangered Rivers and the Conservation Movement,* he received the Lifetime Achievement Award from American Rivers, the nation's principal river saving organization, in 1988. He spends most winters in Kelly, Wyoming, at the upper reaches of the Columbia watershed.

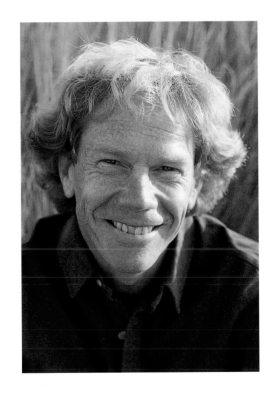